I Can Make That!

I Can Make That!

Fantastic Crafts for Kids

Mary Wallace

MAPLE
TREE
PRESS

Maple Tree Press Inc.
51 Front Street East, Suite 200, Toronto, Ontario M5E 1B3
www.mapletreepress.com

Distributed in Canada by Raincoast Books
9050 Shaughnessy Street, Vancouver, British Columbia V6P 6E5

Distributed in the United States by Publishers Group West
1700 Fourth Street, Berkeley, California 94710

Cataloguing in Publication Data
Wallace, Mary, 1950–
   I can make that!: fantastic crafts for kids / Mary Wallace.

ISBN 1-897066-33-3

   1. Handicraft—Juvenile literature. I. Title.

TT160.W354 2005   j745.5   C2004-904659-4

Design & art direction: Julia Naimska and Word & Image Design (www.wordandimagedesign.com)
Photography: Mary Wallace

We acknowledge the financial support of the Canada Council for the Arts, the Ontario Arts
Council, the Government of Canada through the Book Publishing Industry Development
Program (BPIDP), and the Government of Ontario through the Ontario Media Development
Corporation's Book Initiative for our publishing activities.

ONTARIO ARTS COUNCIL
CONSEIL DES ARTS DE L'ONTARIO

Printed in China

C   D   E   F

I Can Make...

Costumes

Puppets

Nature Crafts

Toys

Games

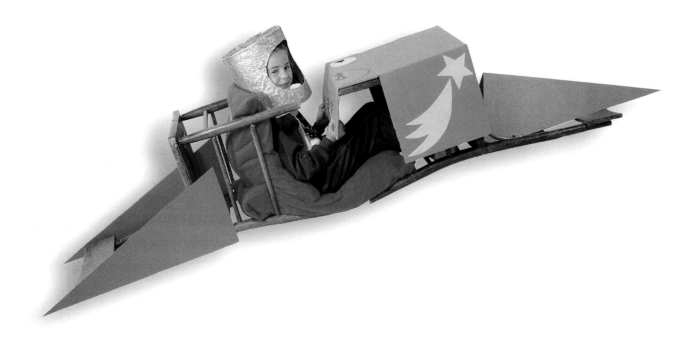

Costumes

LET'S MAKE COSTUMES

You can make and wear all the costumes in this book. It's fun—and easy! These two pages show the things used to make the costumes you'll see in this chapter. You can use other things too if you like. You'll find most of what you need around your own home. Always get permission to use what you find.

- safety pins
- rope
- crayons
- tempera paint
- aluminum foil
- Bristol board
- polyester stuffing
- stocking
- sweat suit
- cardboard box

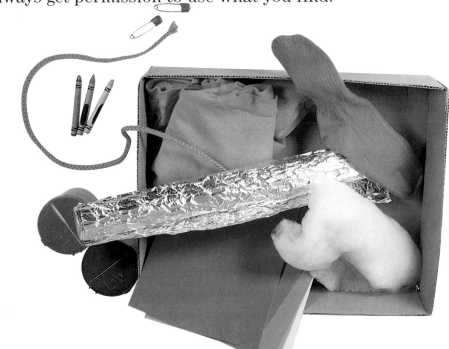

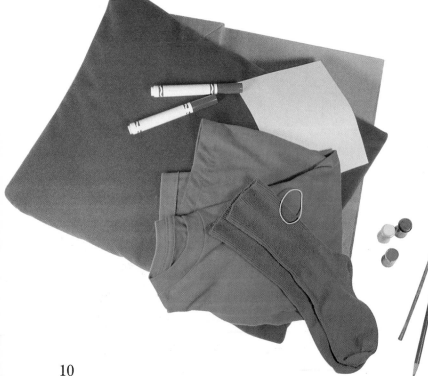

- pencil
- twist tie
- food coloring
- socks
- rubber band
- T-shirt
- markers
- tracing paper
- pillow
- paper bag

- metal paper fasteners
- corrugated cardboard
- colored tape
- hole punch
- plastic bags
- straws
- bath towel
- bowl
- cornstarch
- self-adhesive vinyl

- spoon
- shortening
- paintbrush
- yarn
- ice-cube tray
- paint stir stick
- masking tape
- colored paper
- paper tube
- acrylic paint

- fabric
- stretch pants
- newspaper
- white glue
- tape
- stapler
- scissors
- chalk
- ribbon

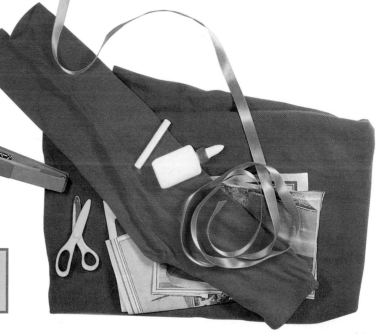

Hint: When stapling rings to fit around head, cover the inside surface with tape to keep staples from poking or catching.

JUST FOR FUN

If it was just for fun, think of who you could become . . .
Look around your house to find some things you could use to change the way
you look. Even the smallest changes in the way you look can make you feel like
a different person. So use your imagination and have fun dressing up!

Find some buttons, yarn, twist ties
and a safety pin and make a necklace,
a ring and a brooch.

Wrap up a ponytail and push in some straws.
Blow up balloons and fasten to straws with
twist ties.

An old hat becomes special with colorful flowers made from plastic bags.

Polyester stuffing glued on an old T-shirt looks like fur trim.

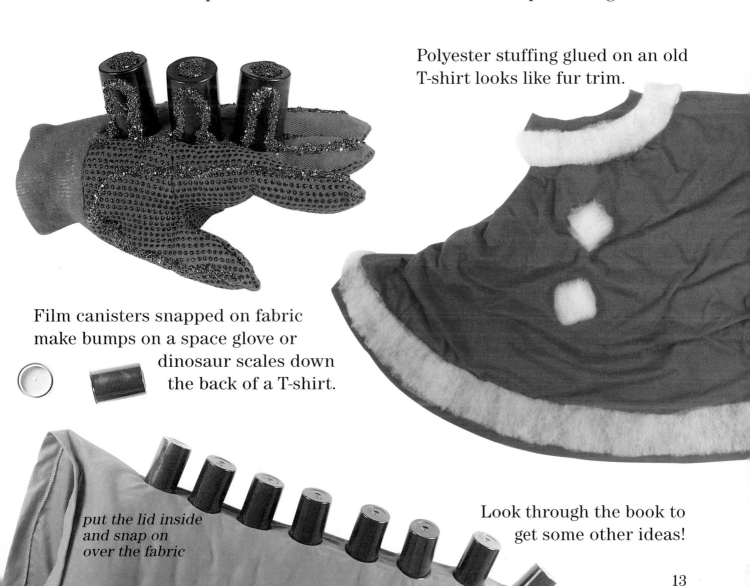

Film canisters snapped on fabric make bumps on a space glove or dinosaur scales down the back of a T-shirt.

put the lid inside and snap on over the fabric

Look through the book to get some other ideas!

13

SUPERHEROES

- large piece of knit fabric
- chalk
- scissors
- Bristol board
- colored tape
- stapler
- *decorate as you like*

CAPE

1 draw outline of cape with chalk

knit fabric

add lines for ties as shown

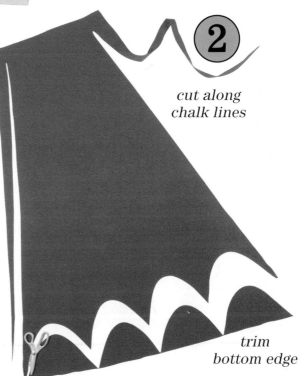

2 cut along chalk lines

trim bottom edge

MASK

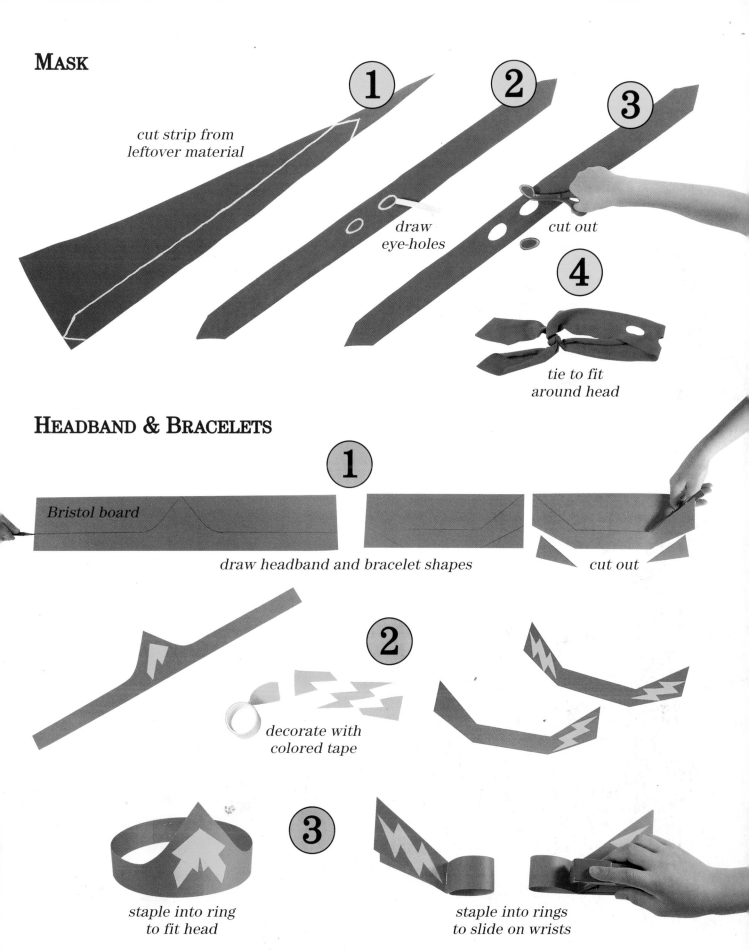

cut strip from
leftover material

draw
eye-holes

cut out

tie to fit
around head

HEADBAND & BRACELETS

Bristol board

draw headband and bracelet shapes

cut out

decorate with
colored tape

staple into ring
to fit head

staple into rings
to slide on wrists

For belt see p. 29.

When stapling ring, see p. 11.

PAPER BAG VEST

- large brown paper bag
- crayons
- scissors
- *decorate as you like*

1 *crinkle paper bag and smooth it out*

repeat until bag is soft

2

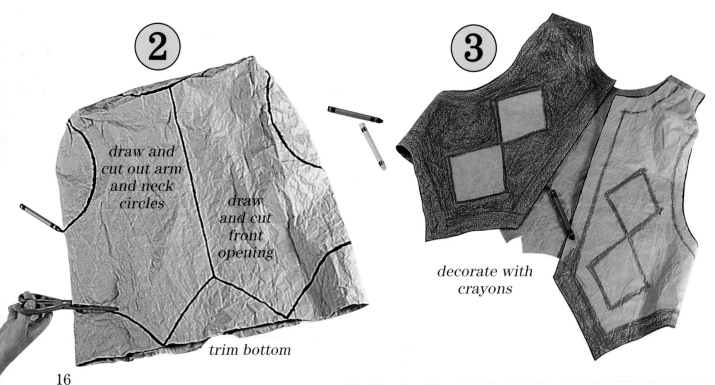

draw and cut out arm and neck circles

draw and cut front opening

trim bottom

3 *decorate with crayons*

ORANGE SMILE

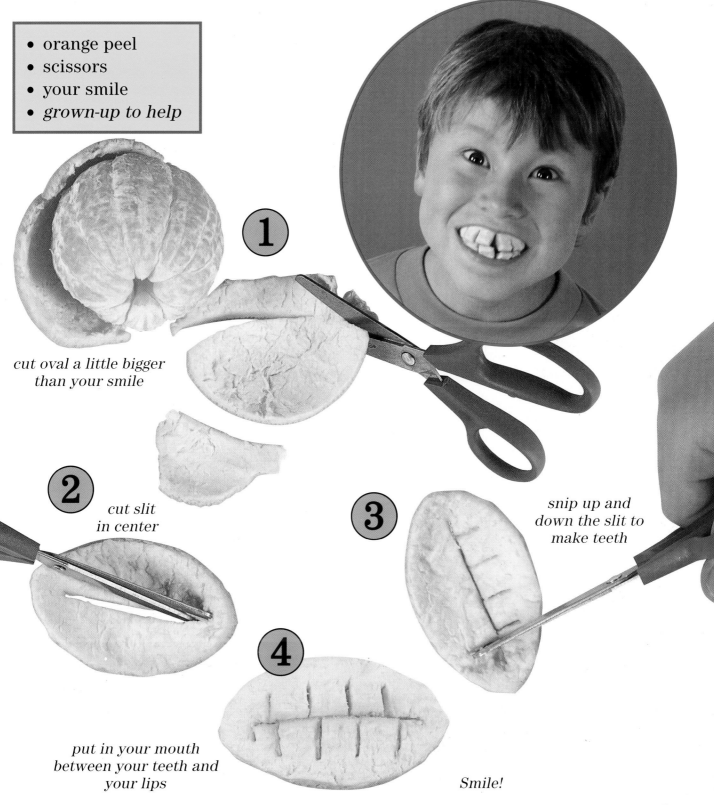

- orange peel
- scissors
- your smile
- *grown-up to help*

1 cut oval a little bigger than your smile

2 cut slit in center

3 snip up and down the slit to make teeth

4 put in your mouth between your teeth and your lips

Smile!

STAR EXPLORER

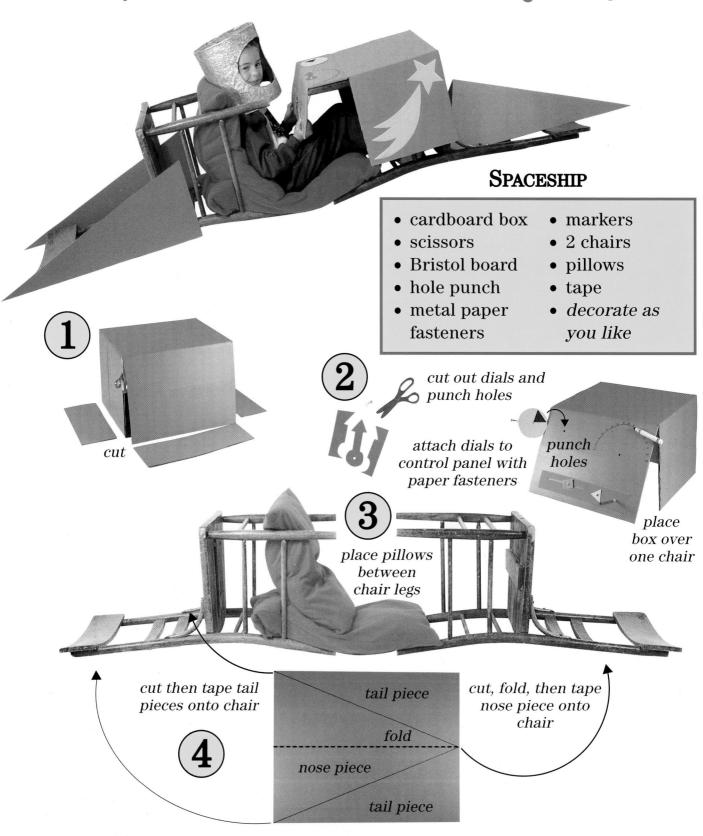

SPACESHIP

- cardboard box
- scissors
- Bristol board
- hole punch
- metal paper fasteners
- markers
- 2 chairs
- pillows
- tape
- *decorate as you like*

1 cut

2 cut out dials and punch holes

attach dials to control panel with paper fasteners

punch holes

place box over one chair

3 place pillows between chair legs

4 cut then tape tail pieces onto chair

tail piece

fold

nose piece

tail piece

cut, fold, then tape nose piece onto chair

SPACE HELMET

- container to fit over your head
- scissors
- aluminum foil
- tape
- *grown-up to help*

1 cut holes for shoulders

cut viewing hole

2 cover with aluminum foil

3 poke foil through holes and fold edges in

secure edges with tape

SPACE ALIEN

- Bristol board
- scissors
- stapler
- tape

1 cut 3 strips of Bristol board

staple short strips as shown

2 cut pieces from Bristol board and staple or tape on

staple long strip into ring to fit head

decorate as you like

For carton like the one shown, ask at an ice cream parlor.
When stapling ring, see p. 11.

19

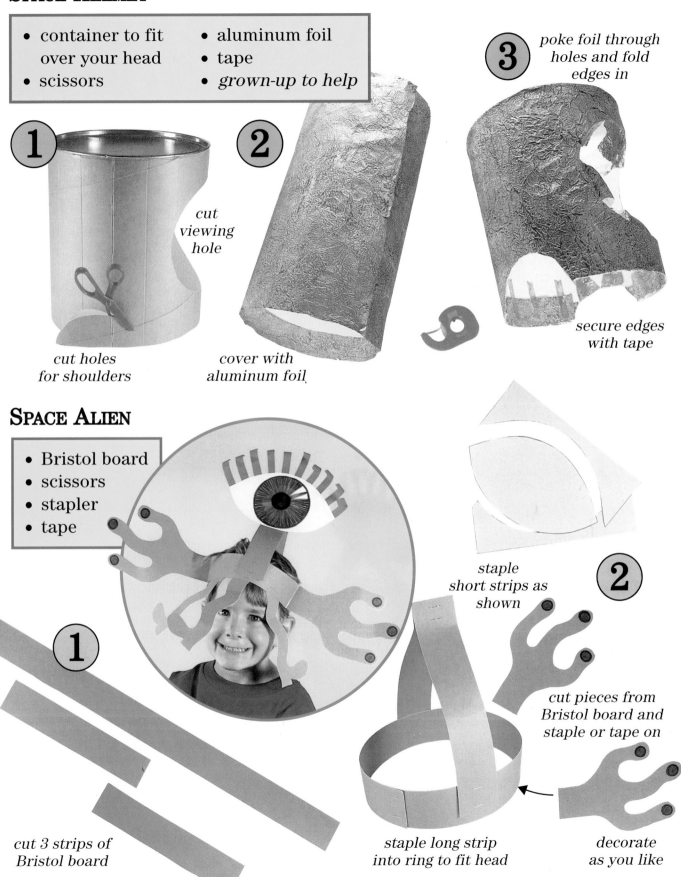

FACE PAINT FUN

- 1 spoonful of soft shortening
- 2 spoonfuls of corn starch
- bowl
- spoon
- ice-cube tray
- food coloring
- paintbrush
- warm water
- *grown-up to help*

1 mix shortening and corn starch

 put some in one tray section for each color

3 add food coloring until you get the color you want

mix with spoon

blue + red = purple
blue + yellow = green
yellow + red = orange
yellow + red + blue = black

TIGER FACE

1

be careful
near eyes

dip finger
in warm water,
then in face
paint

for details use a
paintbrush dipped
in warm water

2

paint orange and white with your finger

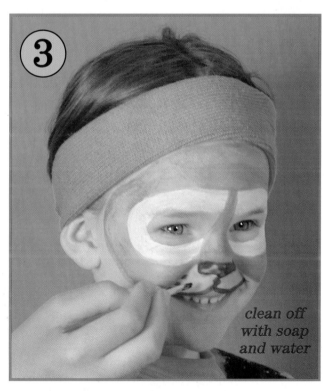

3

clean off
with soap
and water

add black details with paintbrush

For tiger costume, see p. 25.

DRESS-UP ZOO

REINDEER

- Bristol board
- stapler
- pencil
- paper
- scissors

1

staple Bristol board strip into ring to fit head

2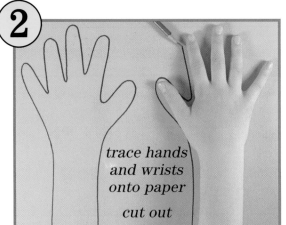

trace hands and wrists onto paper

cut out

3

staple antlers to front of ring

4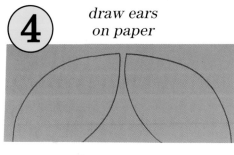

draw ears on paper

cut out

5

staple to sides of ring

22

Mouse

- Bristol board
- stapler
- pencil
- paper
- scissors
- clear tape
- hole punch
- yarn
- rope
- large safety pin

Ears

1 staple Bristol board strip into ring to fit head

2 draw ears on paper

3 staple to ring

cut out

Nose

1 cut paper as shown

2 roll into cone and tape

3 punch 2 holes

cut 2 pieces of yarn to fit around head

4 thread yarn through and knot

tape on yarn whiskers

reinforce with tape

Tail

pin rope tail in place

When stapling, see p. 11.

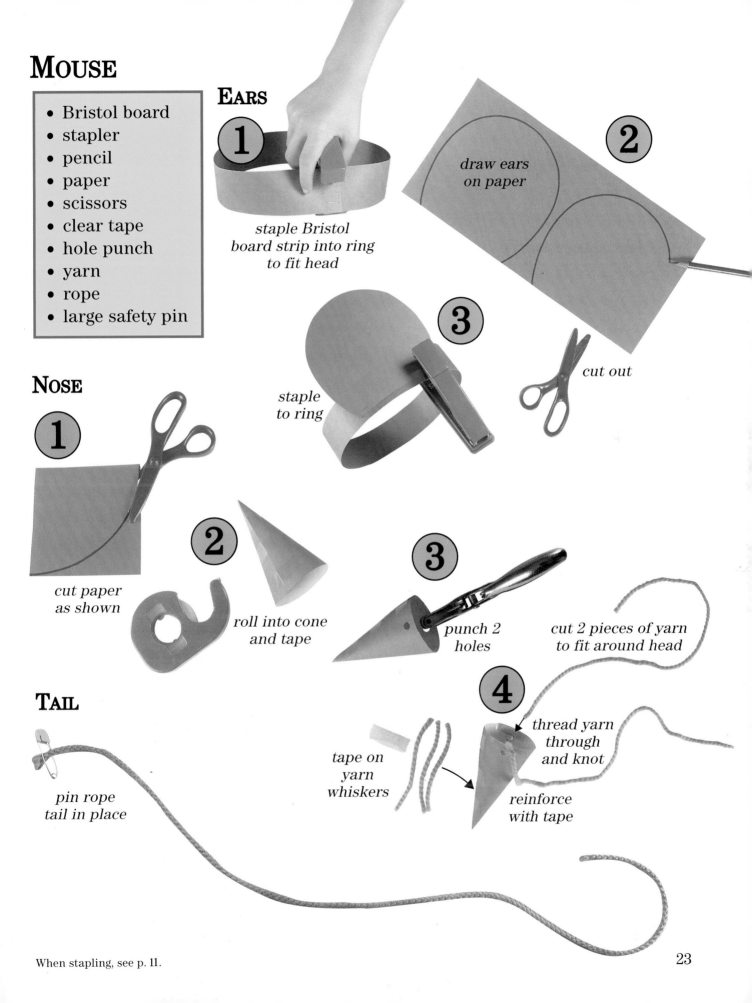

RABBIT

- Bristol board
- stapler
- pencil
- scissors
- 3 plastic bags
- twist tie
- large safety pin
- socks
- fabric paint

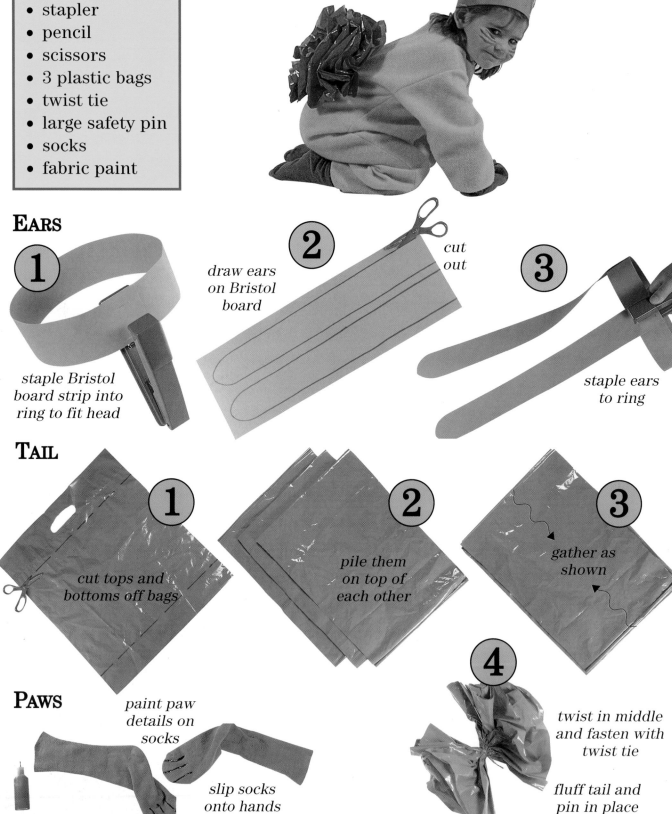

EARS

1 staple Bristol board strip into ring to fit head

2 draw ears on Bristol board · cut out

3 staple ears to ring

TAIL

1 cut tops and bottoms off bags

2 pile them on top of each other

3 gather as shown

4 twist in middle and fasten with twist tie

fluff tail and pin in place

PAWS

paint paw details on socks

slip socks onto hands

24

When stapling, see p. 11.

TIGER

- Bristol board
- pencil
- scissors
- stapler
- hole punch
- yarn
- stocking
- polyester stuffing
- large safety pin
- old sweatsuit
- acrylic paint and brush
- newspapers
- *grown-up to help*

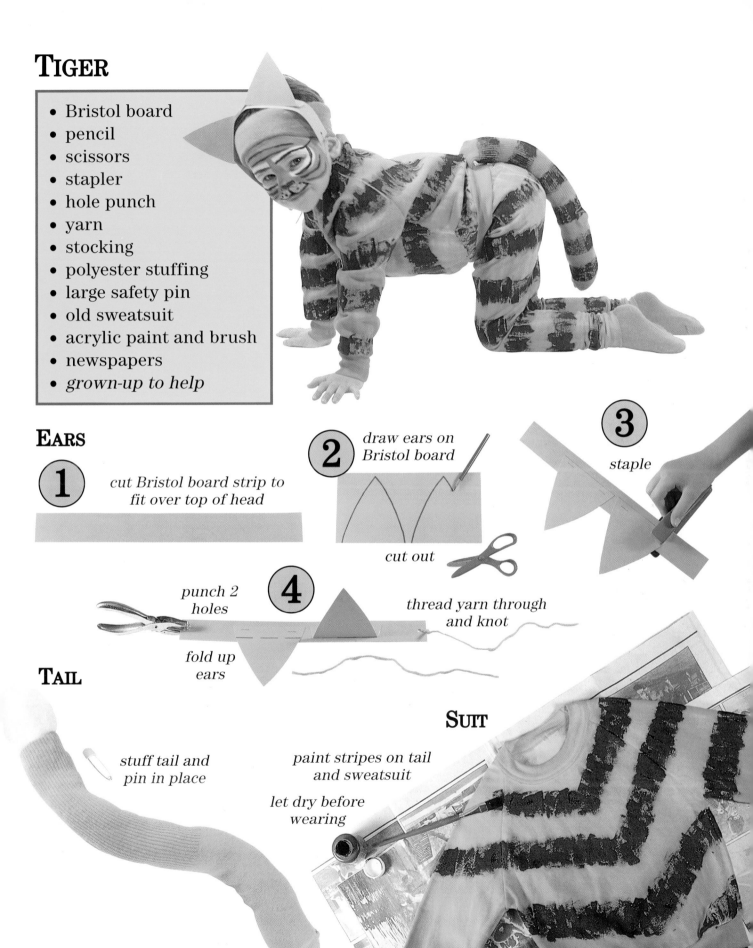

EARS

1 *cut Bristol board strip to fit over top of head*

2 draw ears on Bristol board

cut out

3 staple

4 punch 2 holes

fold up ears

thread yarn through and knot

TAIL

stuff tail and pin in place

SUIT

paint stripes on tail and sweatsuit

let dry before wearing

For face paint, see p. 20.

JOLLY JESTER

- Bristol board
- paper
- glue
- stapler
- scissors
- pair of stretch pants
- tape
- cardboard box that fits over your body
- pencil
- ribbon
- hole punch

WIG

①

glue paper strips onto Bristol board strip

let dry

② staple into ring to fit head

trim bangs

curl paper strips by pulling between thumb and closed scissors

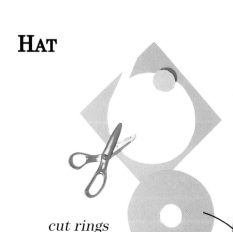

③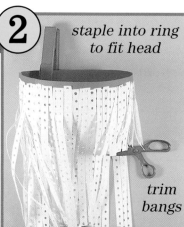

HAT

slip a ring on each leg of stretch pants

knot to hold ring on

cut rings from Bristol board

26

For face paint, see p. 20.

When stapling ring, see p. 11.

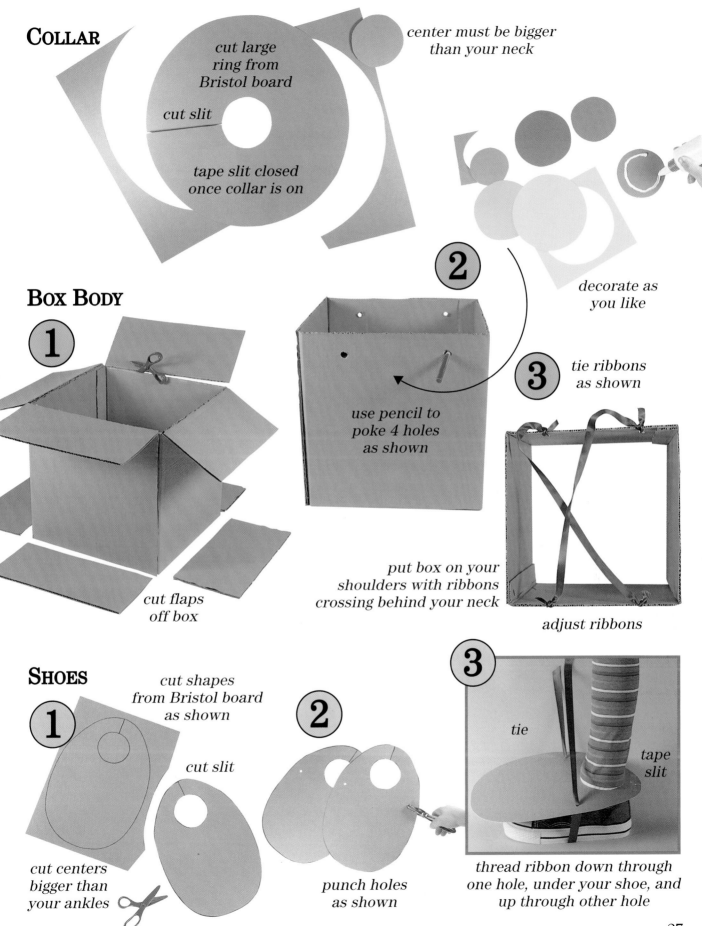

Collar

cut large ring from Bristol board

center must be bigger than your neck

cut slit

tape slit closed once collar is on

decorate as you like

Box Body

1

cut flaps off box

2

use pencil to poke 4 holes as shown

3

tie ribbons as shown

put box on your shoulders with ribbons crossing behind your neck

adjust ribbons

Shoes

cut shapes from Bristol board as shown

1

cut centers bigger than your ankles

cut slit

2

punch holes as shown

3

tie

tape slit

thread ribbon down through one hole, under your shoe, and up through other hole

27

ROBIN HOOD

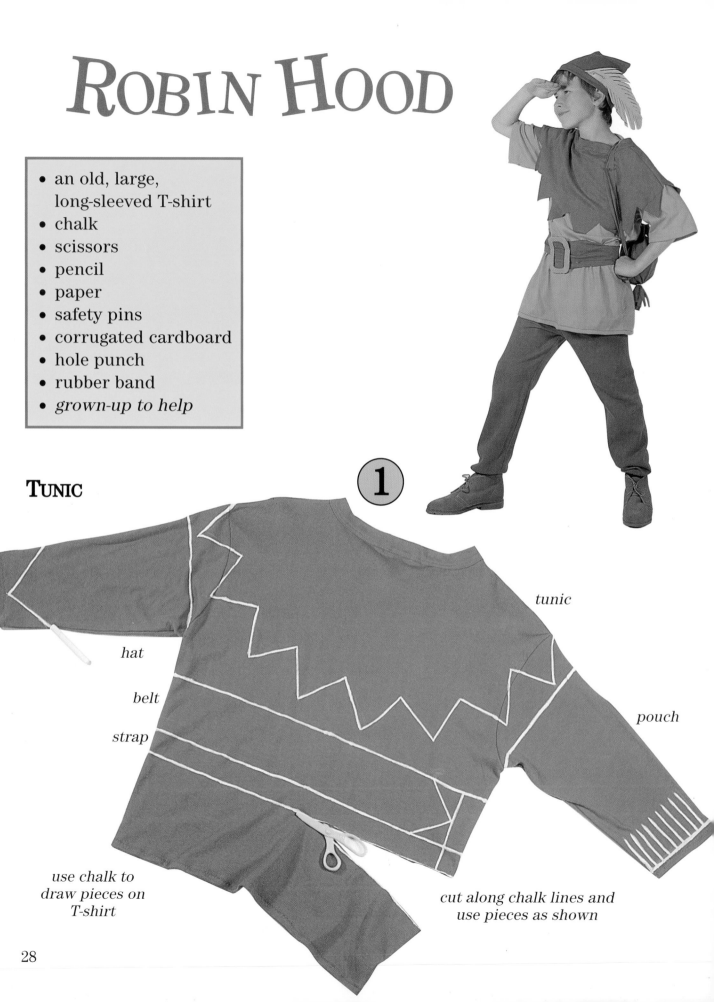

- an old, large, long-sleeved T-shirt
- chalk
- scissors
- pencil
- paper
- safety pins
- corrugated cardboard
- hole punch
- rubber band
- *grown-up to help*

TUNIC

①

hat

belt

strap

tunic

pouch

use chalk to draw pieces on T-shirt

cut along chalk lines and use pieces as shown

HAT

1 use hat piece

2 roll up bottom

3 draw feather on paper — cut out

4 pin onto hat

BELT

1 cardboard — draw buckle shape

2 cut out — punch 4 holes

3 cut slits

4 thread belt piece through slits

5 fold straight end back and pin

6 run pointed end through and pull snug

POUCH

1 use pouch piece and snip 6 holes — cut fringe

2 thread strap piece in and out of holes — gather above fringe with rubber band

3 pull to close — knot

TOGA PARTY

GRECIAN ROBE

- 2 large pieces of fabric
- scissors
- ribbon

 1 fold a piece of fabric in half

cut slit for neck

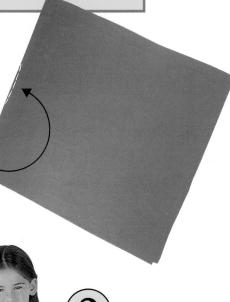 **2** tie one piece of ribbon at waist

 **3** drape fabric on head and tie ribbon around it

tie sleeves up with ribbon

criss-cross a piece of ribbon across chest as shown and tie at back

For jewellery, see p. 12.

ROMAN TUNIC

- bath towel
- piece of rope

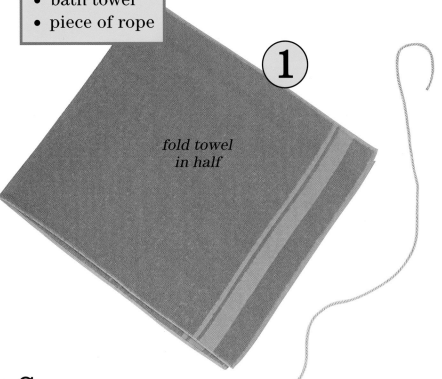

fold towel in half

2

place over shoulder

tie rope around waist

SANDALS

- corrugated cardboard
- pencil
- scissors
- hole punch
- 2 long ribbons

trace your feet on cardboard

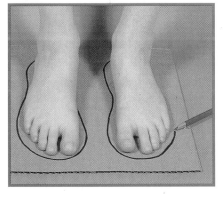

2

cut out

punch holes as shown

3

thread ribbon as shown

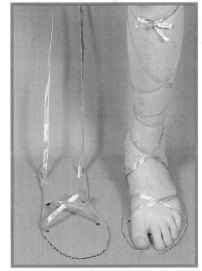

put feet in sandals and lace up around legs

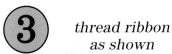

MAGIC MAKER

- large piece of fabric
- ribbon
- pencil
- Bristol board
- scissors
- self-adhesive vinyl
- paint stir stick
- tape
- ribbons

ROBE

fold fabric in half

cut slit for neck

tie one piece of ribbon at waist

decorate with vinyl stars

STARS

1

draw circle on Bristol board

mark 5 dots as shown

connect dots to make star

cut out

2

cut out stars and peel off backing

trace pattern onto self-adhesive vinyl

HAT

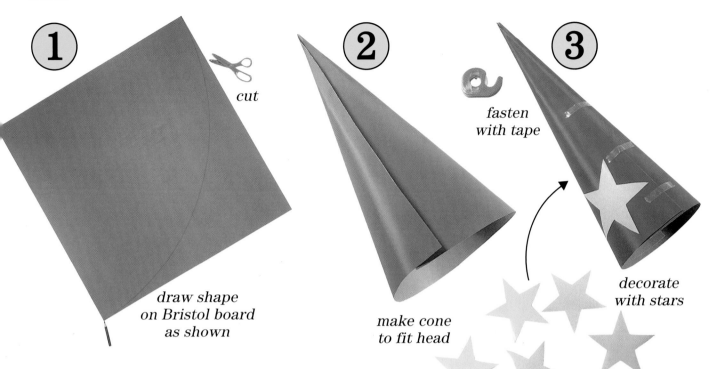

1 cut

draw shape
on Bristol board
as shown

2 make cone
to fit head

3 fasten
with tape

decorate
with stars

MAGIC WAND

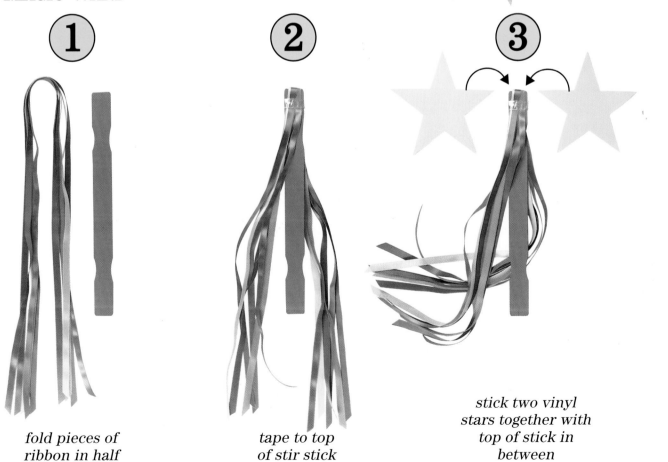

1 fold pieces of
ribbon in half

2 tape to top
of stir stick

3 stick two vinyl
stars together with
top of stick in
between

FIT FOR ROYALTY

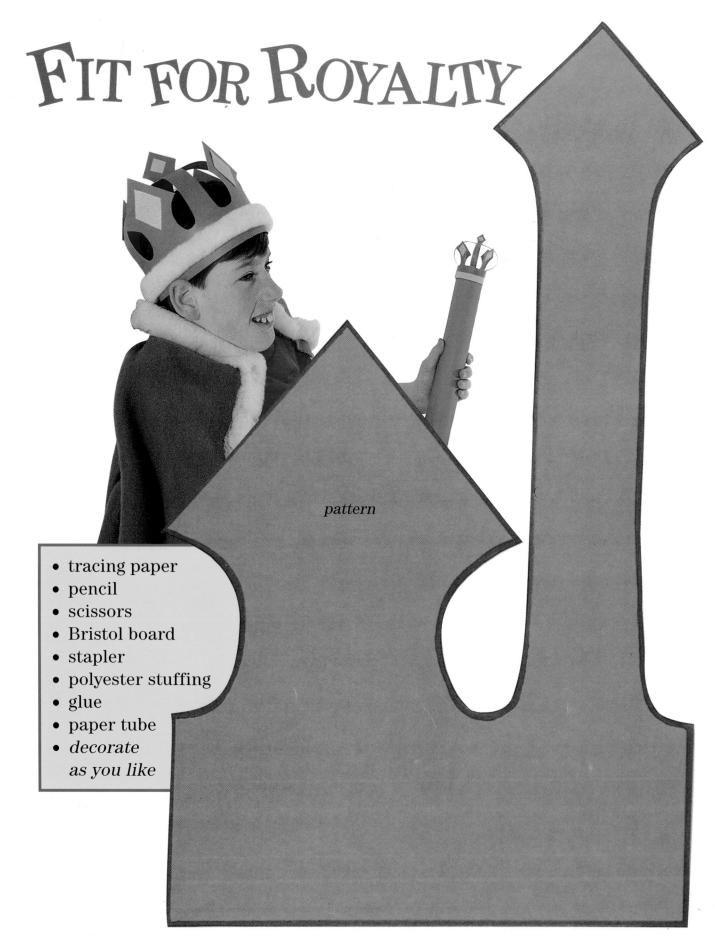

pattern

- tracing paper
- pencil
- scissors
- Bristol board
- stapler
- polyester stuffing
- glue
- paper tube
- *decorate as you like*

34

For cape, see p. 14.

CROWN

1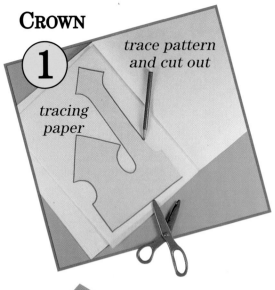

tracing paper

trace pattern and cut out

2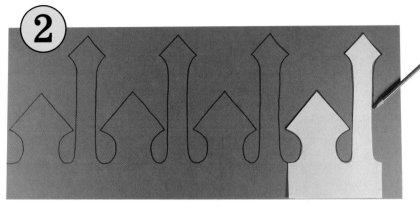

trace outline onto Bristol board 4 times as shown
and cut out

3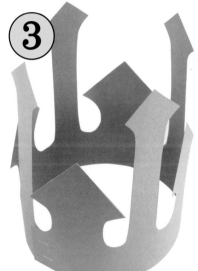

staple
into circle to
fit head

4

overlap 2 opposite
tall strips and staple
flat as shown

5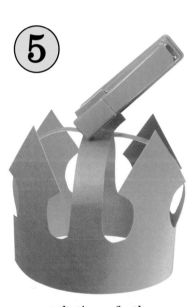

match tips of other
2 tall strips and staple
upright as shown

6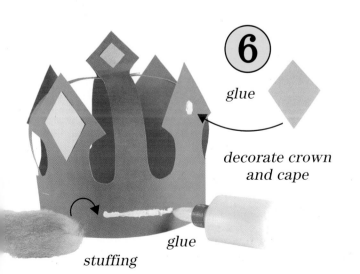

glue

decorate crown
and cape

glue

stuffing

SCEPTER

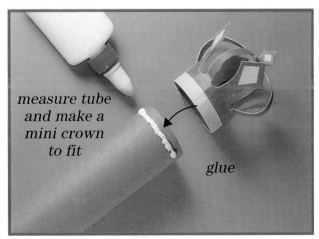

*measure tube
and make a
mini crown
to fit*

glue

When stapling ring, see p. 11.

Enchanted Castle

- 3 cardboard appliance boxes
- Bristol board
- scissors
- tape
- glue
- paper
- 2 drinking straws
- pencil
- rope
- tempera paint
- paintbrush
- *grown-up to help*
- *decorate as you like*

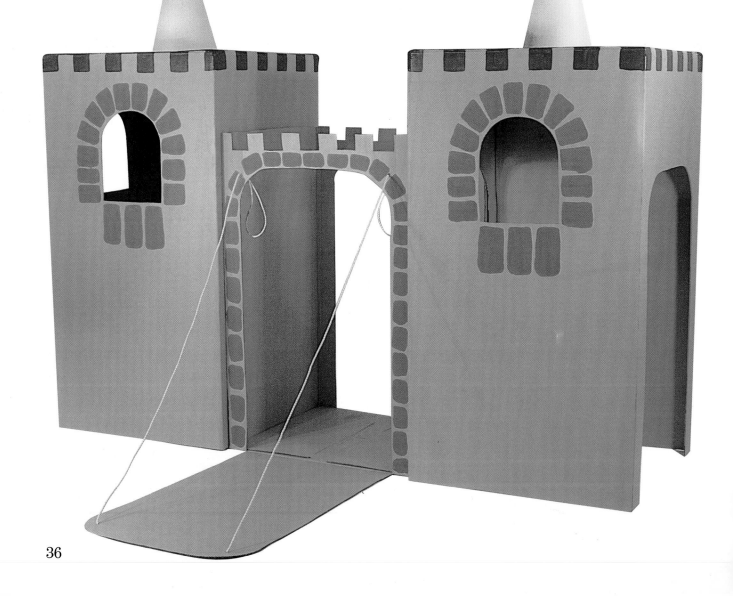

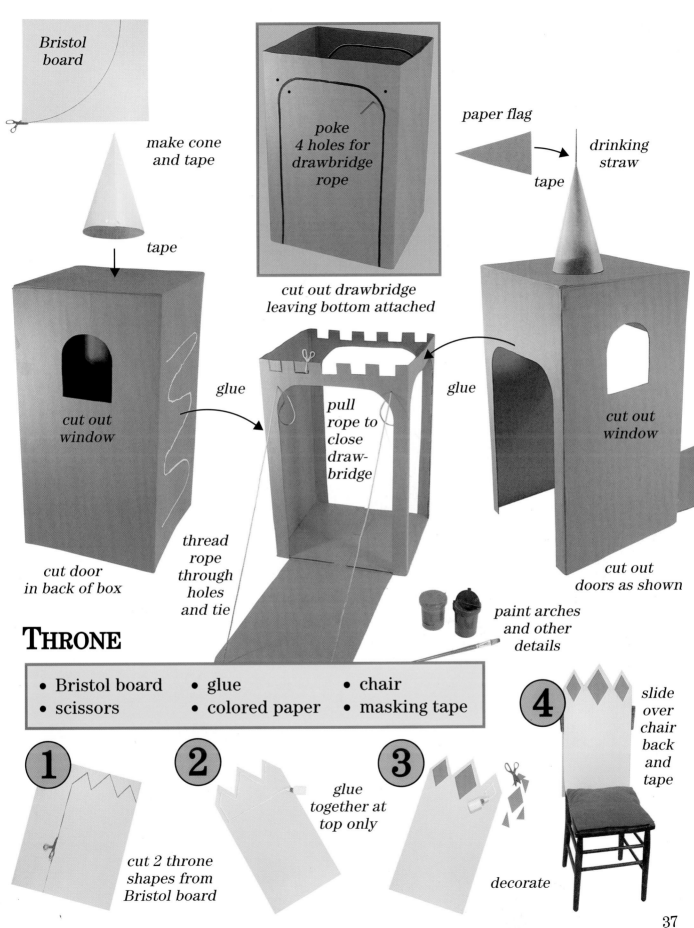

Bristol board

make cone and tape

tape

poke 4 holes for drawbridge rope

cut out drawbridge leaving bottom attached

paper flag

tape

drinking straw

cut out window

cut door in back of box

glue

thread rope through holes and tie

pull rope to close draw-bridge

glue

cut out window

cut out doors as shown

paint arches and other details

THRONE

- Bristol board
- scissors
- glue
- colored paper
- chair
- masking tape

1 cut 2 throne shapes from Bristol board

2 glue together at top only

3 decorate

4 slide over chair back and tape

Puppets

LET'S MAKE PUPPETS

You'll find lots of different puppets you can make in this section of the book. These two pages show what was used to make the puppets you see on the following pages, but you can use other materials you find too. You'll find most things you need around you at home—but don't forget to ask permission to use what you find.

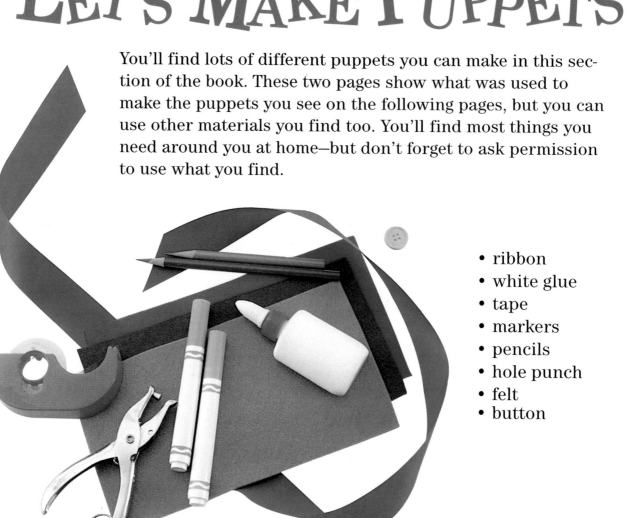

- ribbon
- white glue
- tape
- markers
- pencils
- hole punch
- felt
- button

- sock
- stocking
- aluminum foil
- star stickers
- paint stir stick
- large safety pins
- rubber bands
- yarn
- mittens
- face paint

- paper towels
- sponges
- paper tubes
- cardboard box
- newspaper
- Bristol board
- stapler
- construction paper
- acrylic/fabric paint

- colored paper
- tissue paper
- string
- paper fasteners
- needle and thread
- googly eyes
- scissors
- bottle tops

- footed sleepers
- towel
- small scarf
- face cloth
- T-shirt
- stretchy pants
- polyester stuffing

PUPPET PLAY

Get to Know your Puppet

Every puppet is special. You can give your puppets faces that show how they feel. And when you make them talk and move, they will really come alive!

1. GET YOUR PUPPETS TO TELL ABOUT THEMSELVES

- names
- what they do every day
- favorite things, places, games
- what they like to eat and drink

I like purple pickles and pineapple punch. Let's go out for a picnic lunch!

Hi! I'm Rosie and I love to sing and dance.

2. TWO PUPPETS CAN TALK TO EACH OTHER IN DIFFERENT VOICES

- happy
- angry
- sad
- surprised
- silly
- excited
- scared

Please don't wave your wand and make my treasure disappear!

OK. But only if you'll breathe fire so we can toast marshmallows.

See us run and jump!

3. MAKE YOUR PUPPET MOVE

- bow
- kiss
- twist
- fall
- shake hands
- sleep
- pick things up
- put things down
- move things
- walk
- jump
- run
- chase
- dance
- push
- pull
- nod
- shake
- cry
- laugh

These are some of the ways you can play with your puppets. But we know you can think of more. When you get to know your puppets, there are lots of amazing things they can say and do. Have fun!

Silly Dragon

- *grown-up to help sew*
- Bristol board
- scissors
- white glue
- an old sock
- crumpled newspaper
- 2 rubber bands
- felt
- googly eyes
- needle and thread

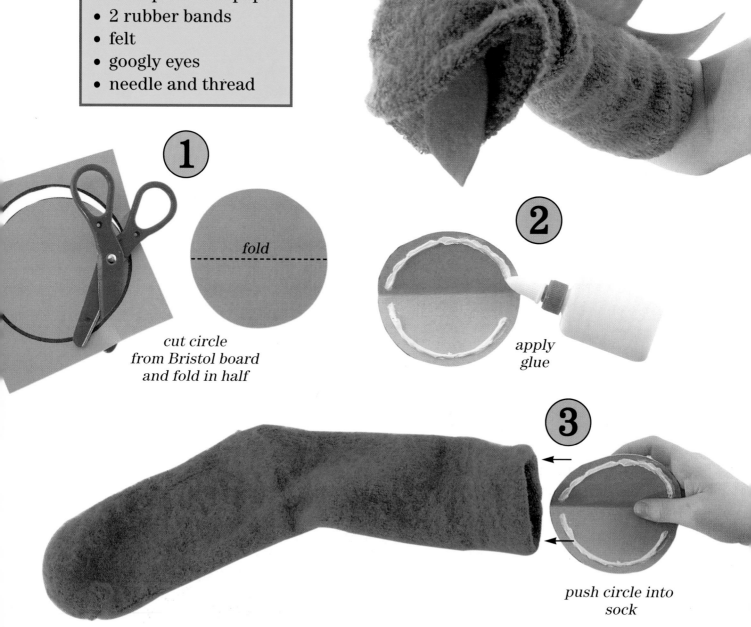

1

fold

cut circle
from Bristol board
and fold in half

2

apply
glue

3

push circle into
sock

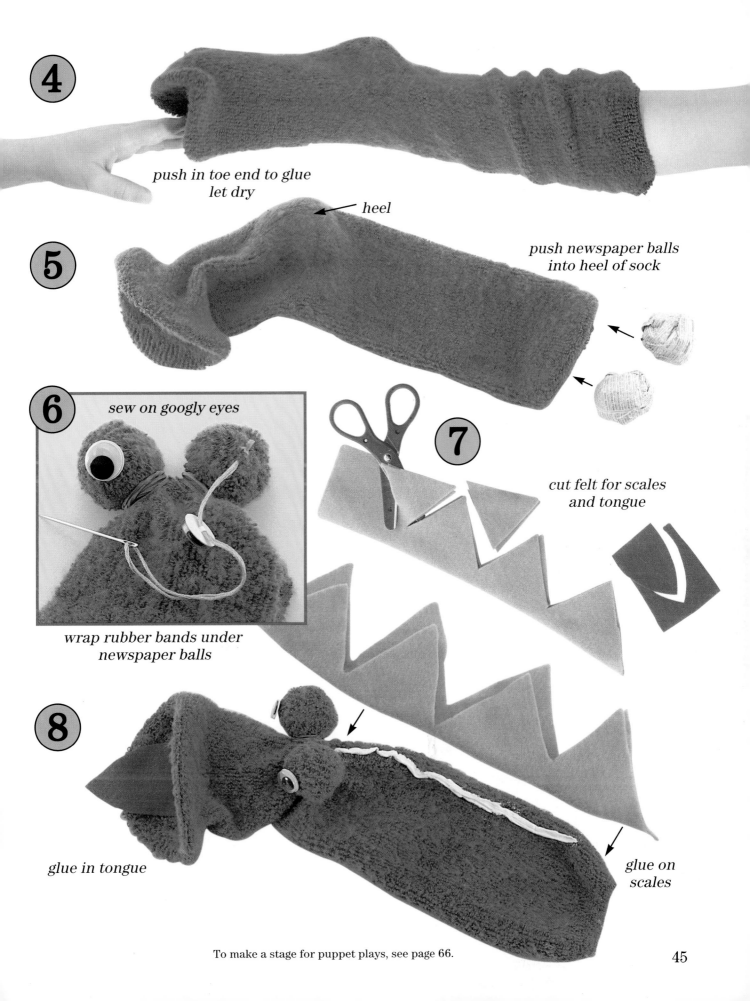

④ push in toe end to glue
let dry

heel

⑤ push newspaper balls
into heel of sock

⑥ sew on googly eyes

wrap rubber bands under
newspaper balls

⑦ cut felt for scales
and tongue

⑧ glue in tongue

glue on
scales

To make a stage for puppet plays, see page 66.

MOUTHY MINIATURES

- your own hands
- washable markers
- bottle tops
- bits of yarn and tissue paper
- scarf

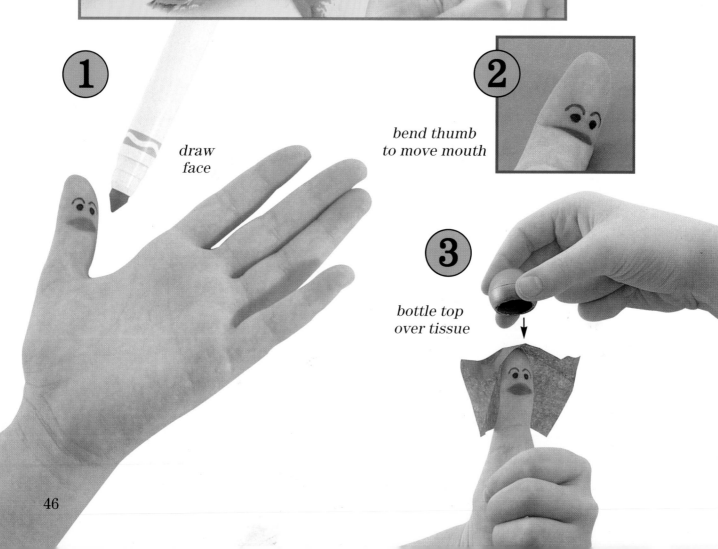

1 *draw face*

2 *bend thumb to move mouth*

3 *bottle top over tissue*

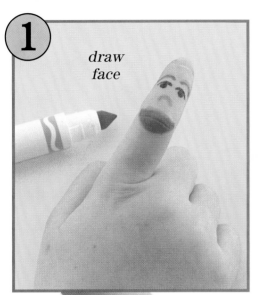

1
draw face

2
place yarn on finger

3
bottle top over yarn

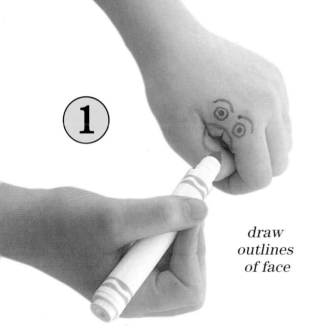

1
draw outlines of face

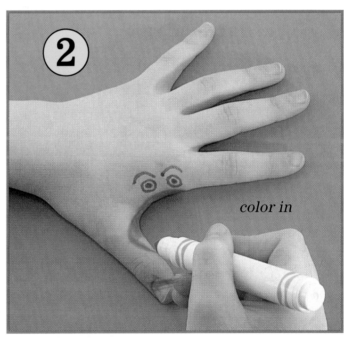

2
color in

3
tie on scarf

move thumb up and down to make puppet talk

WONDERFUL WIZARD

- small paper tube
- scissors
- paper towel
- white glue
- water
- soupspoon
- plastic container
- markers or colored tape
- Bristol board
- tape
- face cloth
- star stickers
- *decorate as you like*

① cut piece of tube

② tear paper towel into pieces

③ mix 3 soupspoons of glue and 3 soup-spoons of water

cover table

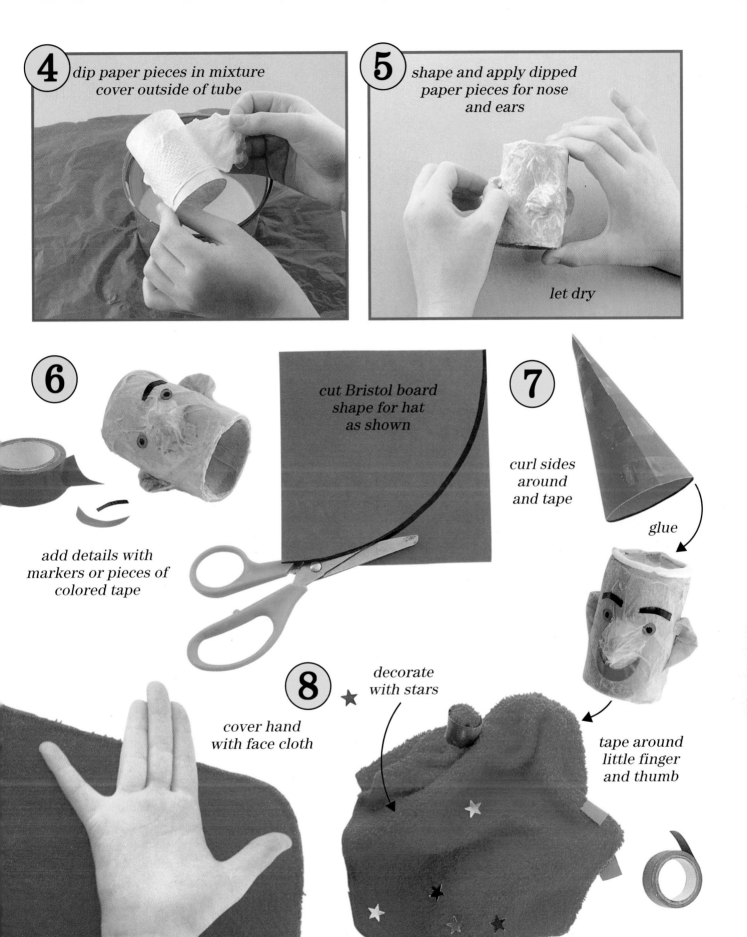

4 dip paper pieces in mixture cover outside of tube

5 shape and apply dipped paper pieces for nose and ears

let dry

6

add details with markers or pieces of colored tape

cut Bristol board shape for hat as shown

7 curl sides around and tape

glue

tape around little finger and thumb

8 cover hand with face cloth

decorate with stars

49

PINK PIG

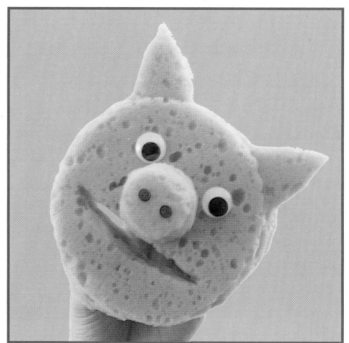

- 2 soft sponges
- marker
- scissors
- white glue
- 2 googly eyes
- fabric paint
- *decorate as you like*

1 draw three lines like this on sponge

2 cut short lines part way through

3 cut long line all the way through

4 try on and adjust cuts

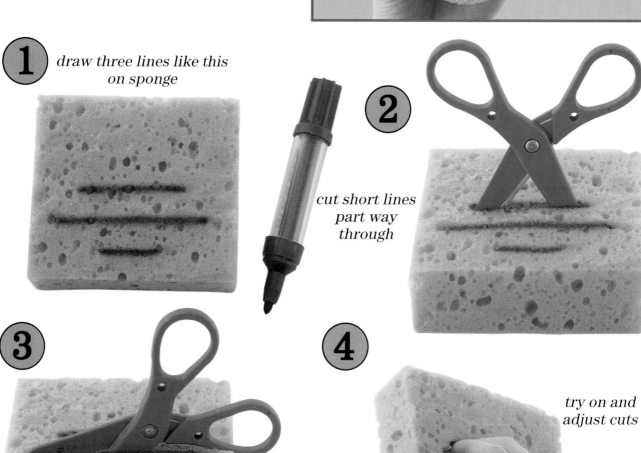

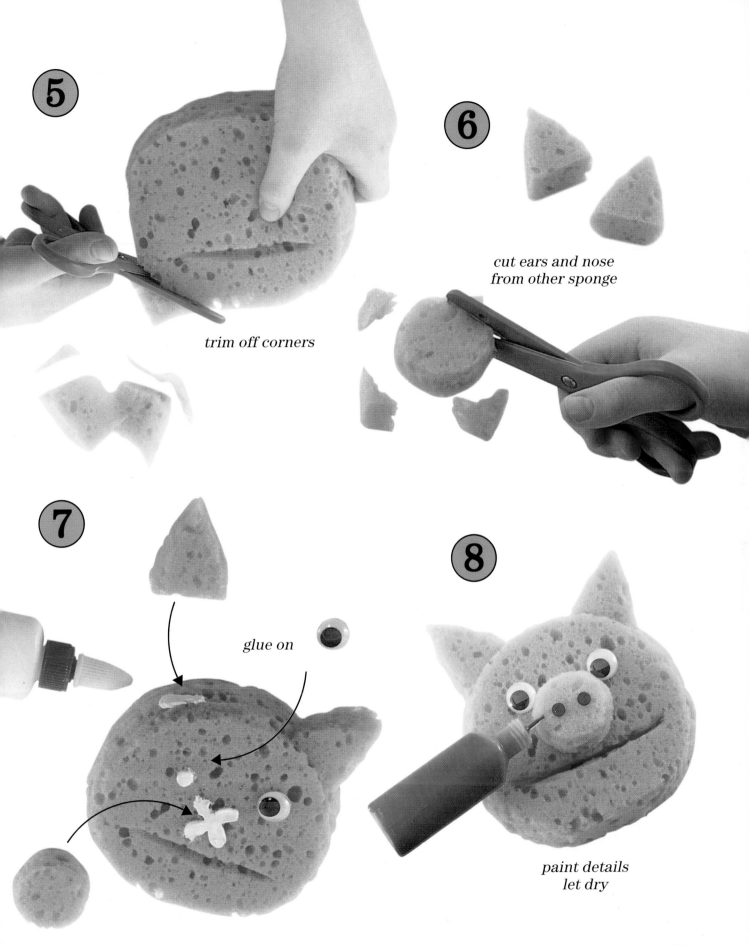

5

trim off corners

6

cut ears and nose
from other sponge

7

glue on

8

paint details
let dry

CHIN CHUCKLER

- your own chin
- washable markers or face paint
- rubber band for long hair
- light-weight scarf or T-shirt
- bed
- *decorate as you like*

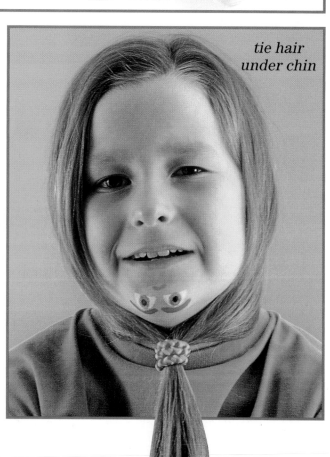

1 *make your chin into an upside-down face*

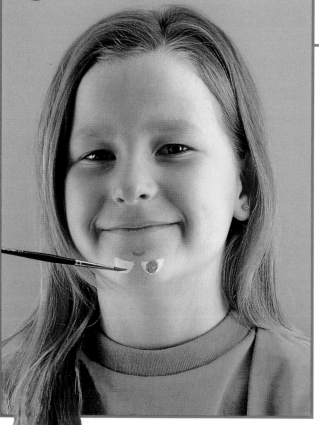

draw eyes and nose

tie hair under chin

2 *cover the top half of your face using T-shirt or scarf*

pull on T-shirt upside-down

wrap scarf loosely and tie in back

3

**lie with your head
hanging over side of bed
and make funny faces
for your friends**

FINGER FRIENDS

- colored construction paper
- scissors
- white glue
- markers
- tape
- *decorate as you like*

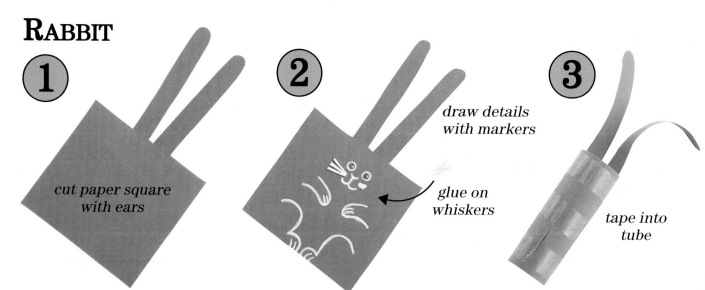

QUEEN

1 cut points for crown

use square a little longer than your finger

2 draw details with markers

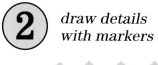

3 tape into tube

RABBIT

1 cut paper square with ears

2 draw details with markers

glue on whiskers

3 tape into tube

MOUSE

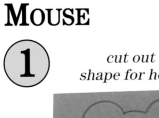

1 *cut out shape for head*

use square
a little longer
than your finger

2 draw details
with markers

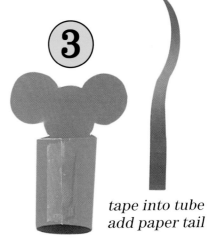

3 tape into tube
add paper tail

MISS MUFFET

1

cut half-way down to
make hair

use rectangle
about twice as long
as your finger

2 draw details with
markers

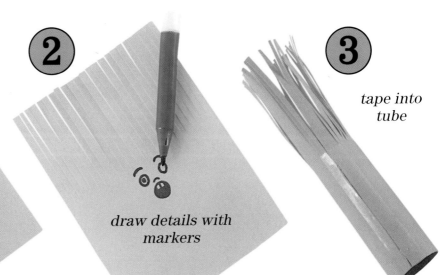

3 tape into
tube

SPIDER

1

use rectangle
a little longer
than your finger

cut 8 legs
leaving strip
on top for ring

2 tape ring

3 glue on
paper eyes

bend
legs

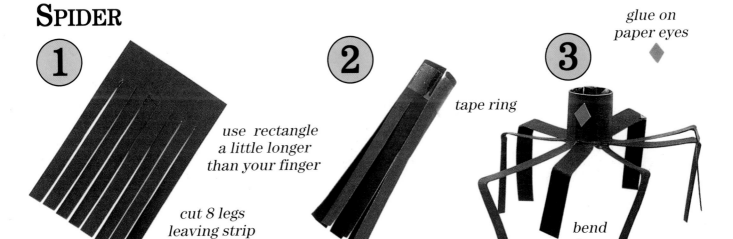

55

BEST BUDDY

- *grown-up to help with sewing*
- cardboard box
- scissors
- an old pair of stretchy pants
- 2 rubber bands
- polyester stuffing
- ribbon
- googly eyes
- footed sleepers
- needle and thread
- mittens

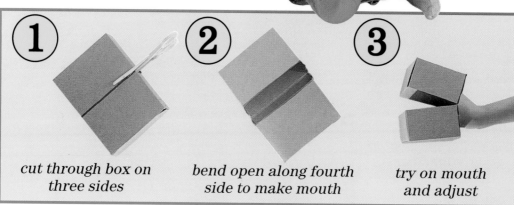

1 cut through box on three sides

2 bend open along fourth side to make mouth

3 try on mouth and adjust

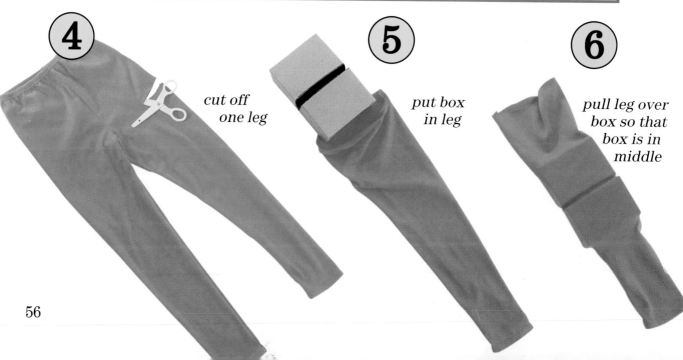

4 cut off one leg

5 put box in leg

6 pull leg over box so that box is in middle

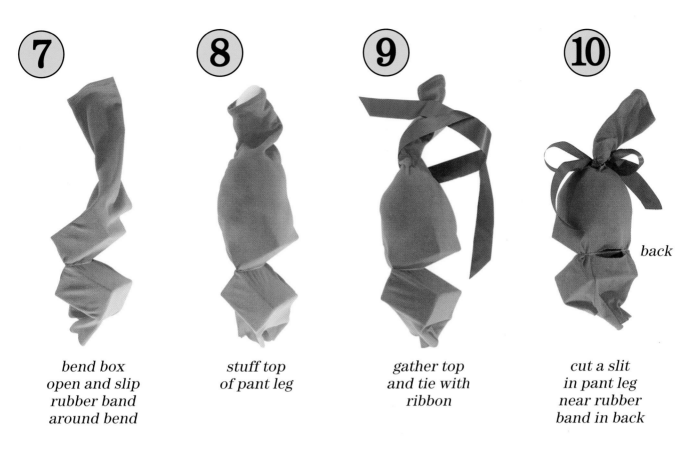

7 bend box open and slip rubber band around bend

8 stuff top of pant leg

9 gather top and tie with ribbon

10 cut a slit in pant leg near rubber band in back

back

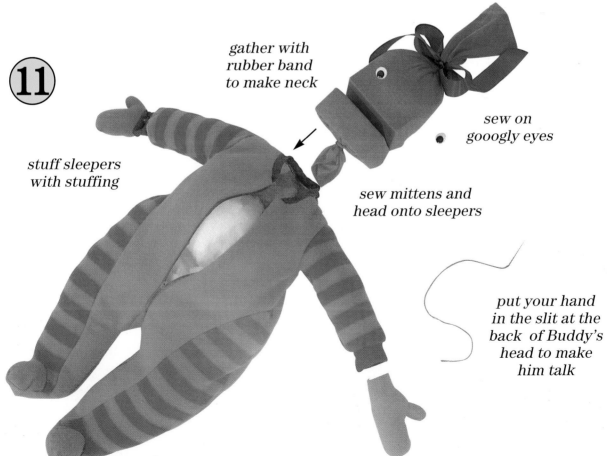

11

gather with rubber band to make neck

stuff sleepers with stuffing

sew mittens and head onto sleepers

sew on gooogly eyes

put your hand in the slit at the back of Buddy's head to make him talk

ROSIE ROCK STAR

- *grown-up to help with stapling*
- paint stir stick
- toilet paper tube
- stocking
- scissors
- 2 rubber bands
- felt
- stapler
- markers
- yarn
- glue
- *decorate as you like*

1 cut foot off stocking

slide tube onto stick

2 pull stocking leg over tube

3 secure stocking ends to stick with rubber bands

4

slide tube down
over rubber band

5

cut hands
from felt

staple
hands
onto
stocking
leg

6 glue yarn
on back

let dry

7 draw
face
with
markers

8

fluff hair

9

hold on
to tube
and bottom
of stick

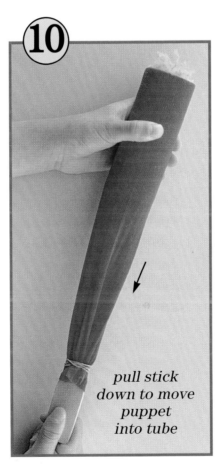

10

pull stick
down to move
puppet
into tube

11

push up
stick to
make Rosie
pop up

Finger Wigglers

- Bristol board
- pencil
- scissors
- tape
- markers
- button
- *decorate as you like*

Gabby Gator

1 *fold*

draw outline

2

add nostrils and teeth

3 *cut out shape*

snip off bottom nostrils

4

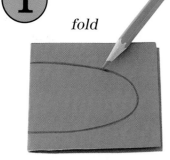

*cut strips for finger rings
include eye bumps on one*

5

tape strips into rings

6 *tape rings to outside
of head*

*fold nostrils
and eyes up*

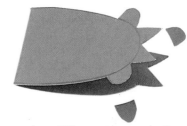

*fold
teeth in*

TWEETER

1 *fold and glue*

cut out bird
and beak

cut strips
for finger rings

2

tape rings to
back of wings

3

move fingers in and
out to flap wings

ELEPHANT

1

draw outline on
Bristol board

2

trace button for holes

3 have a grown-up
help you start the holes

draw details with markers

SUNSHINE

1

cut body
from
Bristol
board

draw
details
with
markers

fold
feet up

2

cut strips for
finger rings

tape into rings

3

tape rings
to back
of legs

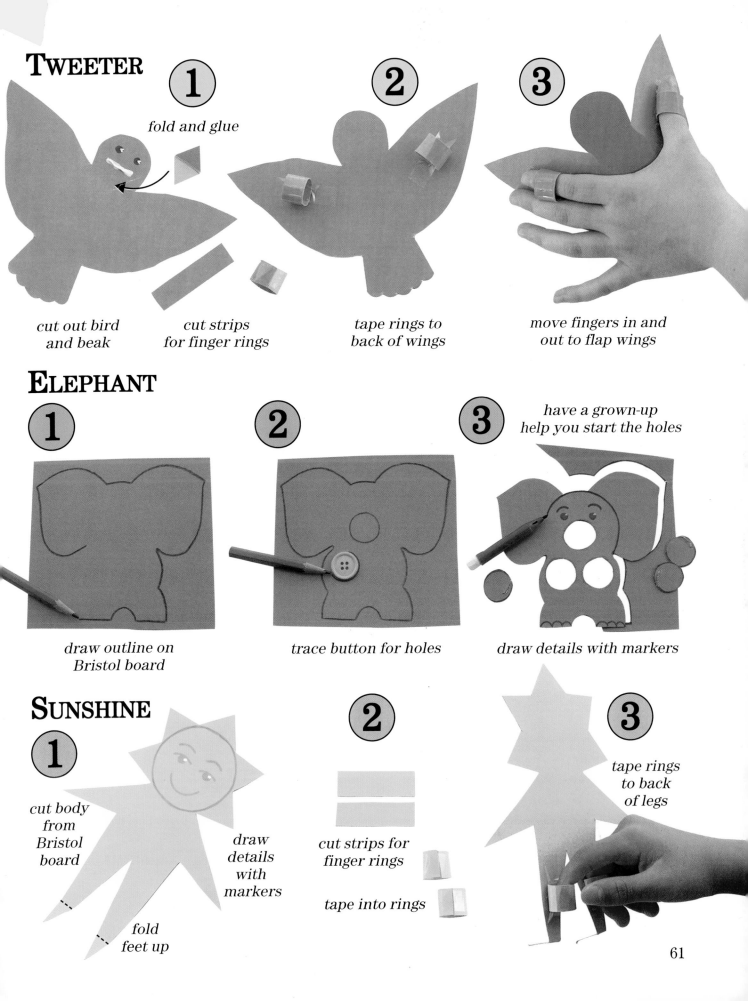

61

STRING KING

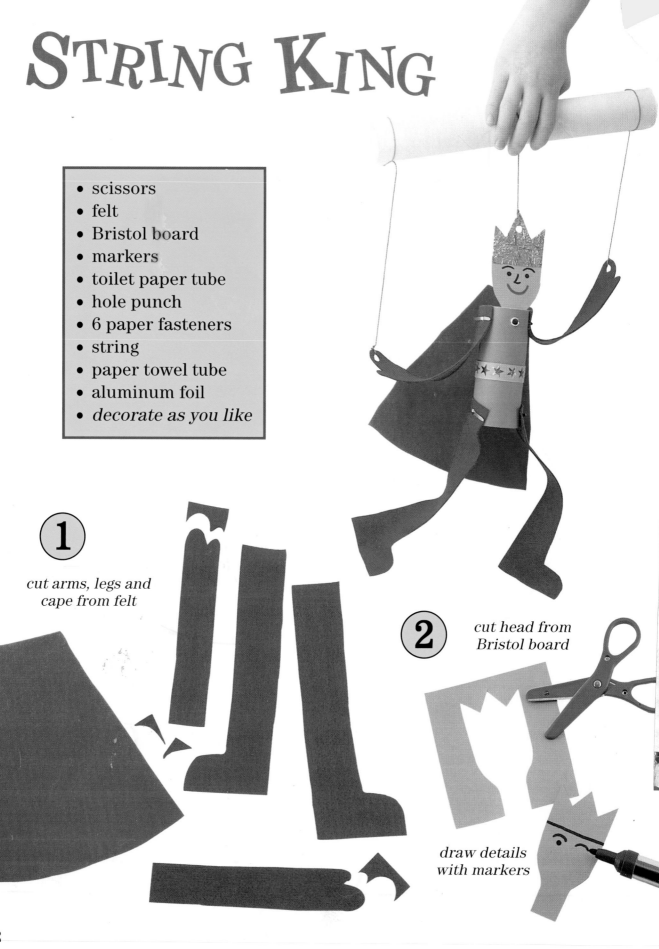

- scissors
- felt
- Bristol board
- markers
- toilet paper tube
- hole punch
- 6 paper fasteners
- string
- paper towel tube
- aluminum foil
- *decorate as you like*

1 cut arms, legs and cape from felt

2 cut head from Bristol board

draw details with markers

3

punch holes
as shown

punch
6 holes
in tube as
shown

4

push paper fasteners
through from
inside of tube

attach
arms and legs
to tube

6

loop and
tie strings
around long
tube

tie string
to ends
of arms and
top of crown

5

attach head
and cape

decorate

To make a horse for your king to ride, see page 64.

PRANCING PONY

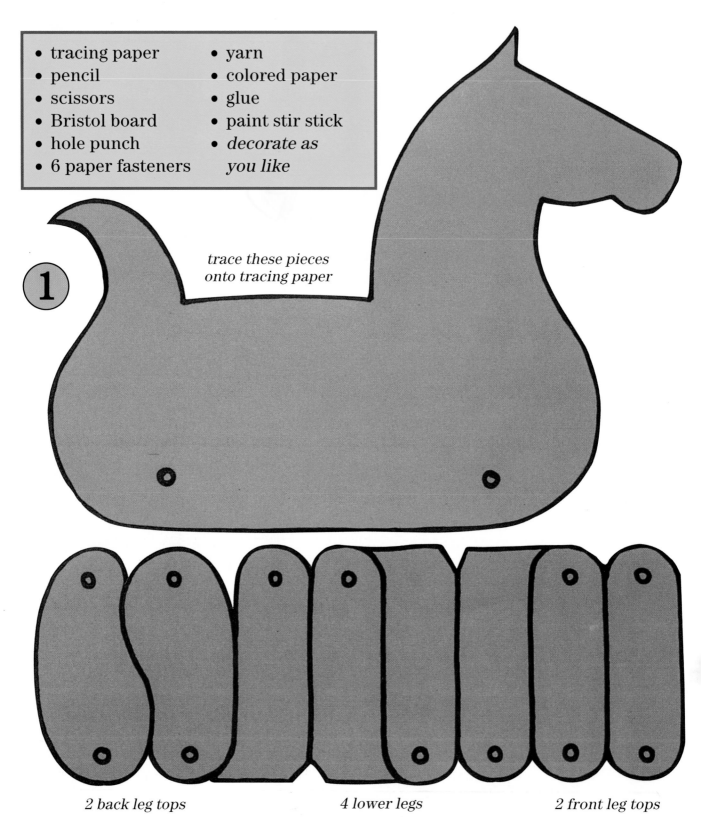

- tracing paper
- pencil
- scissors
- Bristol board
- hole punch
- 6 paper fasteners
- yarn
- colored paper
- glue
- paint stir stick
- *decorate as you like*

①

trace these pieces onto tracing paper

2 back leg tops   *4 lower legs*   *2 front leg tops*

64

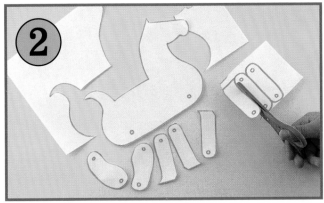

cut out pieces

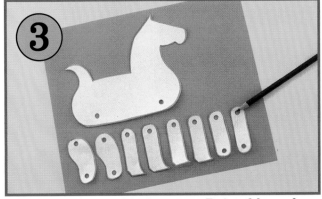

trace shapes and holes onto Bristol board

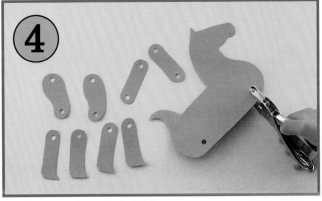

cut out and punch holes

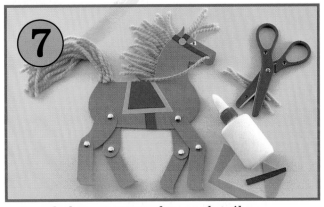

**bend
fastener
ends
loosely**

2 paper fasteners attach leg tops to body

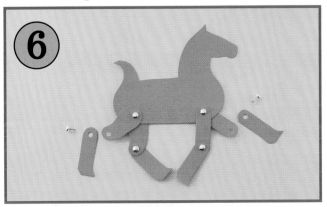

4 paper fasteners attach lower legs to tops

cut and glue paper and yarn details

glue stick on back and let dry

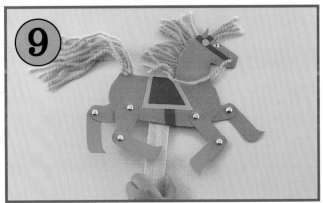

jiggle to make pony prance

To make a stage for puppet plays, see page 66.

PUPPET STAGE

- *grown-up to help with pins*
- 2 chairs
- 4 large towels
- broomstick
- 2 large safety pins
- construction paper
- tape
- markers
- *decorate as you like*

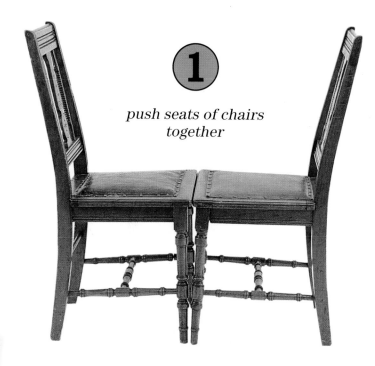

1 push seats of chairs together

2

drape chairs with towels

3 balance broomstick on chair backs

use safety pins to secure towel

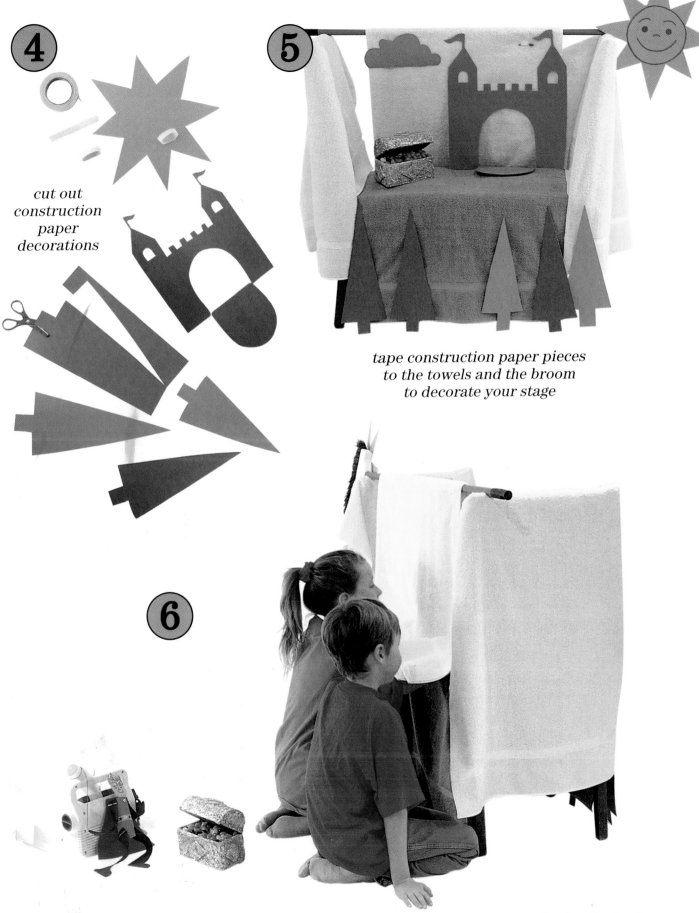

4

cut out construction paper decorations

5

tape construction paper pieces to the towels and the broom to decorate your stage

6

To see how to put on a puppet play, turn the page! 67

PUTTING ON A PUPPET PLAY

- *make puppets talk to each other or the audience*
- *only one puppet speaks at a time*
- *move only the puppet that is speaking*
- *hold the puppet so the audience can see its face*
- *act out a fairy tale or tell a story*

Nature Crafts

LET'S MAKE NATURE CRAFTS

This chapter is filled with amazing crafts you can make. These two pages show the materials used to make the crafts you'll find in this section of the book, but you can use other things too to make your own great crafts. Most things you'll need can be found inside or outside where you live. Always get permission to use what you find. Pick only what you need, enjoy the natural setting, and have fun!

- corn silk
- cornhusks
- shallow bowl
- tempera paint
- cardboard
- googly eyes
- scissors
- crayons
- dandelion stems

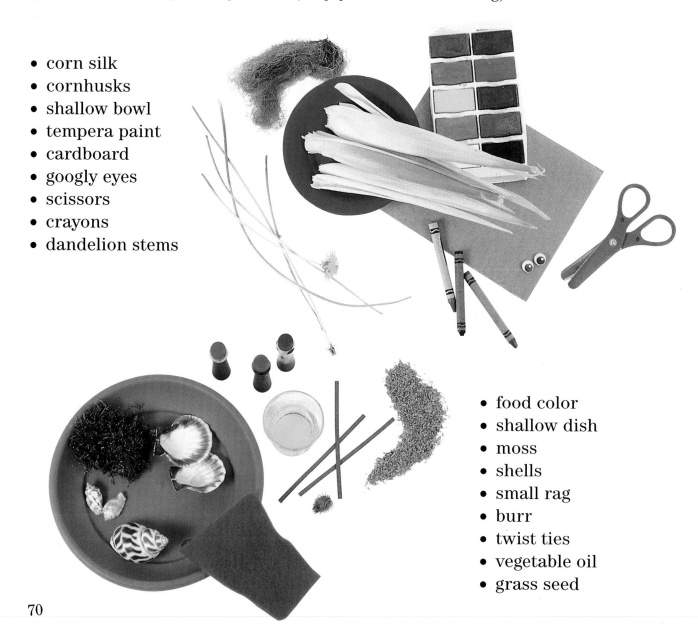

- food color
- shallow dish
- moss
- shells
- small rag
- burr
- twist ties
- vegetable oil
- grass seed

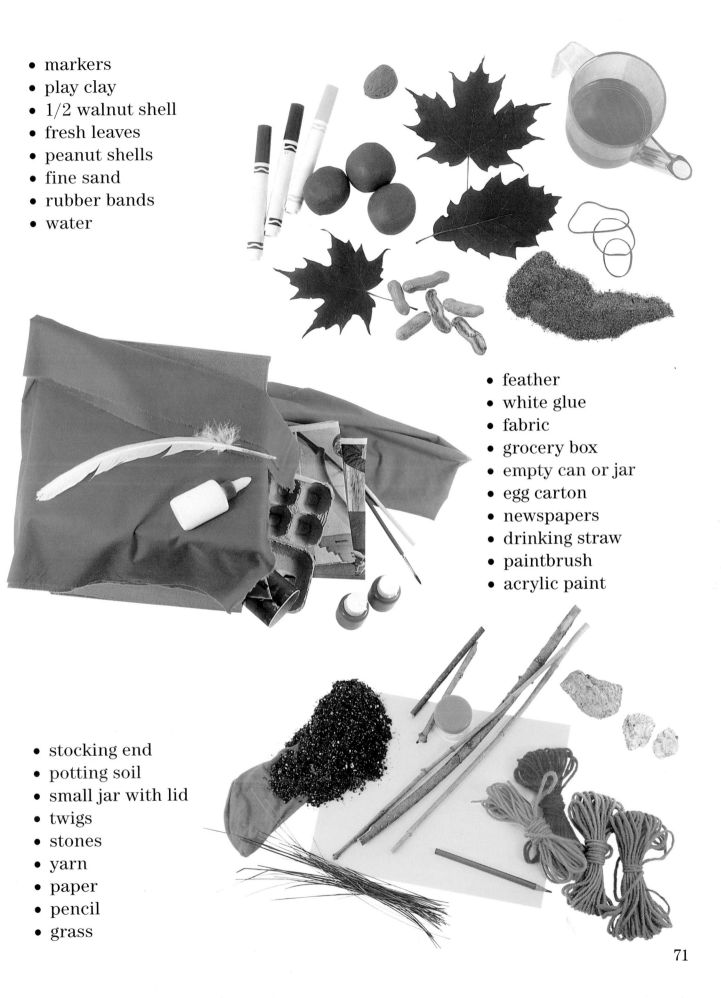

- markers
- play clay
- 1/2 walnut shell
- fresh leaves
- peanut shells
- fine sand
- rubber bands
- water

- feather
- white glue
- fabric
- grocery box
- empty can or jar
- egg carton
- newspapers
- drinking straw
- paintbrush
- acrylic paint

- stocking end
- potting soil
- small jar with lid
- twigs
- stones
- yarn
- paper
- pencil
- grass

71

TWIG VASE

- empty jar or can
- 2 rubber bands
- twigs
- yarn

①

*break twigs about the
same length as the can*

②

*put rubber bands
around the can*

3

pull out rubber
bands and insert
twig as shown

4

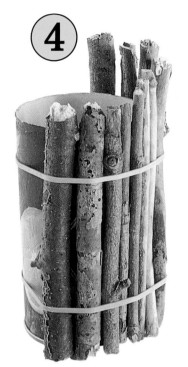

repeat until twigs
cover outside of can

5

wrap and tie yarn to
cover rubber bands

SPIDER

- 4 twist ties
- 1/2 walnut shell
- play clay
- googly eyes

1

line up twist ties
and twist together
in middle

2

place twist
in walnut shell

secure with
a ball of
play clay

3

press on balls
of play clay and
googly eyes

attach spider to vase
with play clay

73

STONE STATUES

- small stones
- 1 spoon of vegetable oil
- bowl
- small rag
- play clay
- *decorate as you like*

1

dip tip of rag in oil and polish surface of stones

wipe off excess oil

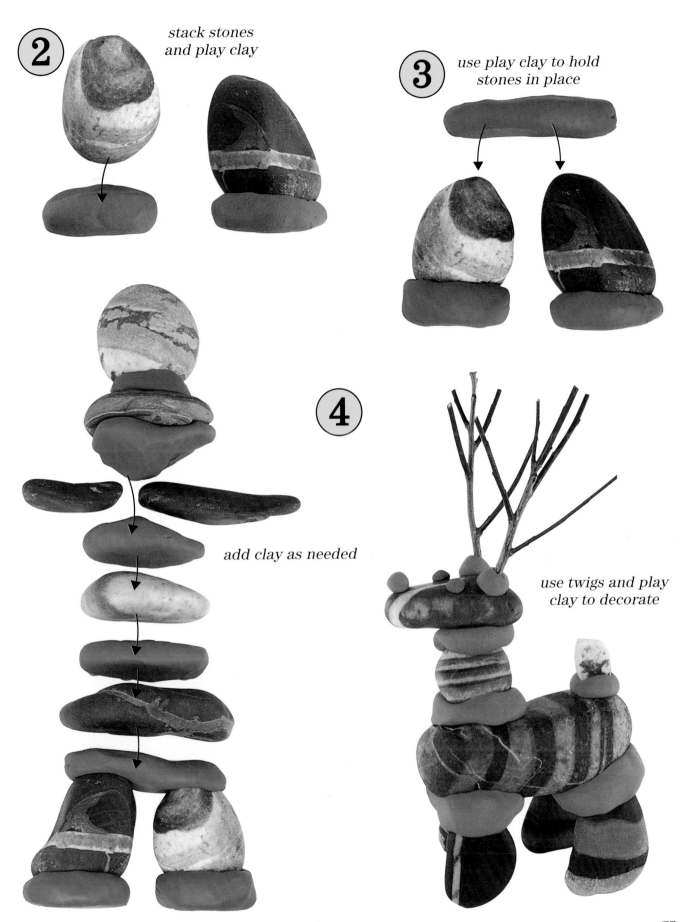

2 *stack stones and play clay*

3 *use play clay to hold stones in place*

4 *add clay as needed*

use twigs and play clay to decorate

GRASSY HEAD

- stocking end
- potting soil
- twist ties
- rubber bands
- 2 googly eyes
- white glue
- 1 spoonful of grass seed
- shallow bowl
- scissors
- water

1

put several handfuls of soil in stocking end

2

shape soil into round head and close with twist tie

back of head

3

pinch soil in stocking to make nose and wrap with rubber band

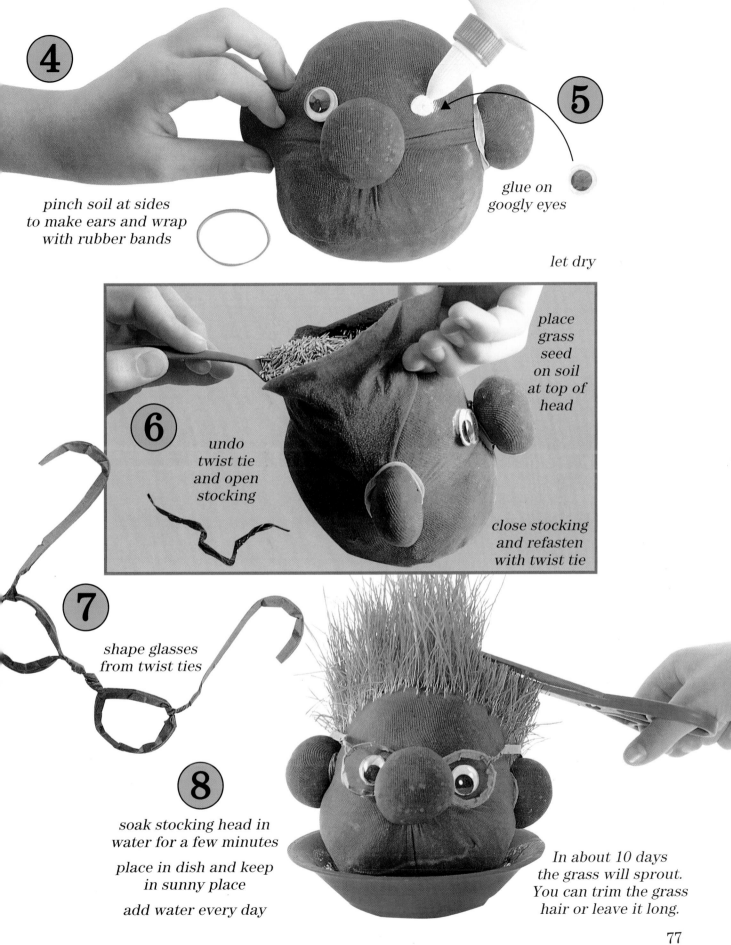

4 pinch soil at sides
to make ears and wrap
with rubber bands

5 glue on
googly eyes

let dry

6 undo
twist tie
and open
stocking

place
grass
seed
on soil
at top of
head

close stocking
and refasten
with twist tie

7 shape glasses
from twist ties

8 soak stocking head in
water for a few minutes

place in dish and keep
in sunny place

add water every day

In about 10 days
the grass will sprout.
You can trim the grass
hair or leave it long.

NUTTY BUDDIES

- peanuts in the shell
- white glue
- twist ties
- scissors
- grass
- markers
- *decorate as you like*

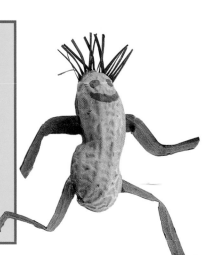

1

crack peanut shell in half

save peanuts to eat later

2

glue along edges of both halves of shell

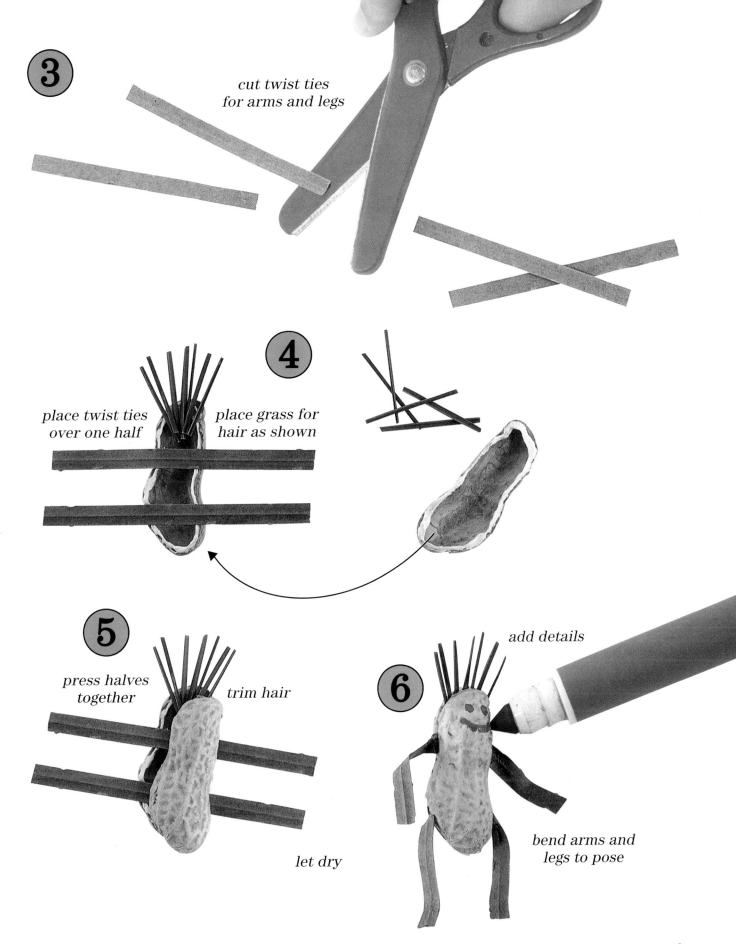

3 cut twist ties
for arms and legs

4

place twist ties
over one half

place grass for
hair as shown

5 press halves
together

trim hair

let dry

6 add details

bend arms and
legs to pose

PRESSED LEAVES

- grocery box
- scissors
- newspapers
- 2 large rubber bands
- tape
- fresh leaves
- *grown-up to help*
- *decorate as you like*

①

*ask a grown-up
to cut 2 pieces of
cardboard from box*

② *decorate as
you like*

③

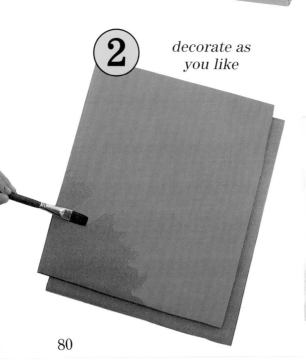

*cut newspapers
to fit between cardboard*

④ stretch 2 rubber bands
around leaf press

tape rubber bands
along one edge

⑤ press leaves between
newspaper

leave 4 sheets of newpaper
between each layer of leaves

close carefully and
use rubber bands
to hold closed

⑥ put closed leaf press
under a pile of books
for about 2 weeks

use pressed leaves
to decorate your other crafts

OLD-TIME WRITING

- found feather
- disinfectant
- scissors
- cardboard
- acrylic paint
- paintbrush
- pressed leaves

- white glue
- small jar with lid
- play clay
- drinking straw
- water
- food color
- *grown-up to help*

QUILL PEN

ask grown-up to clean feather with disinfectant

cut off base at an angle

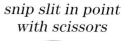 snip slit in point with scissors

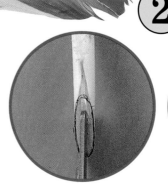

HOLDER

1 cut out circle from cardboard

paint and let dry

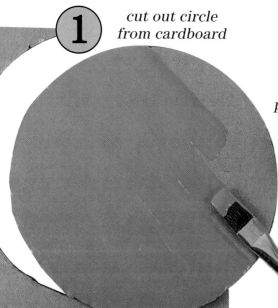

2 glue on pressed leaves

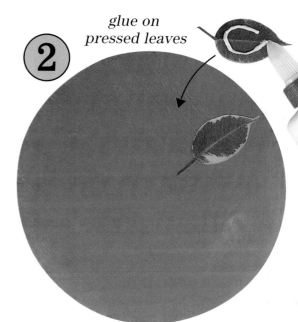

For pressed leaves, see p. 80.

3

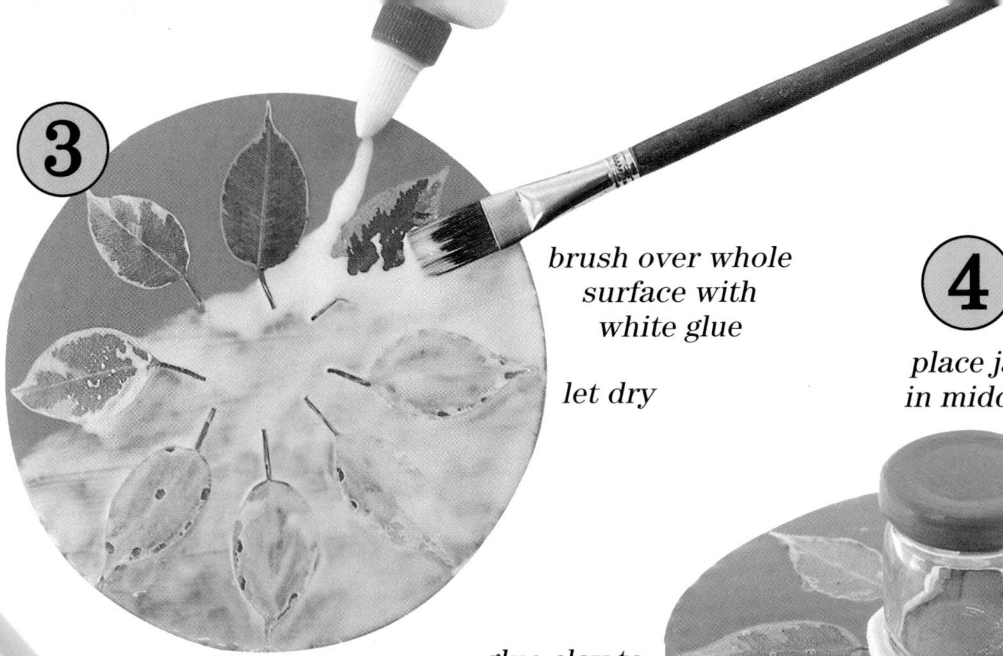

brush over whole
surface with
white glue

let dry

4

place jar
in middle

glue clay to
cardboard
around base
of jar

5

cut piece of straw
to hold pen

6

glue down
piece of clay
and press
in straw

INK

pour water and
food color into jar

dip tip of quill pen
then write

Hi

keep dipping
as you write

GRASS WHISTLE

- a strong blade of grass
- your hands

1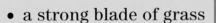

*pick a sturdy
blade of grass*

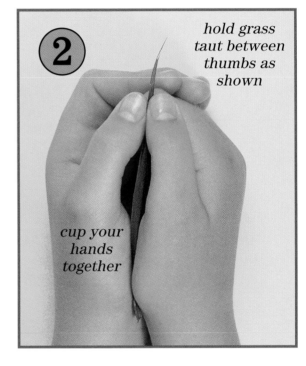

2 *hold grass
taut between
thumbs as
shown*

*cup your
hands
together*

3

*press your lips against your
thumbs and blow hard*

DANDELION LOOPS

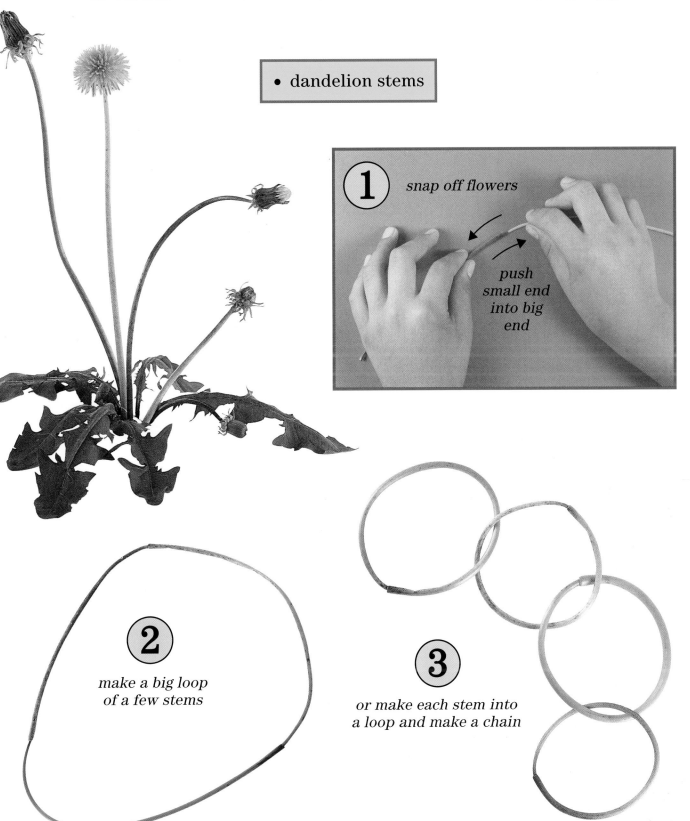

- dandelion stems

1 snap off flowers

push small end into big end

2 make a big loop of a few stems

3 or make each stem into a loop and make a chain

BURR BUTTERFLY

- paper
- pencil
- scissors
- crayons
- burr
- white glue
- *decorate both sides as you like*

①

fold paper in half

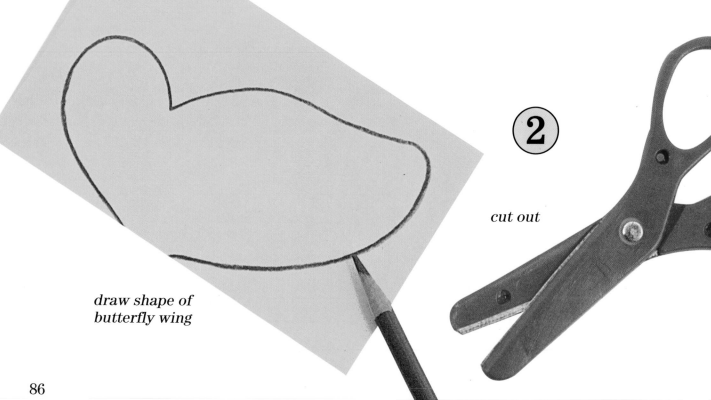

②

cut out

draw shape of butterfly wing

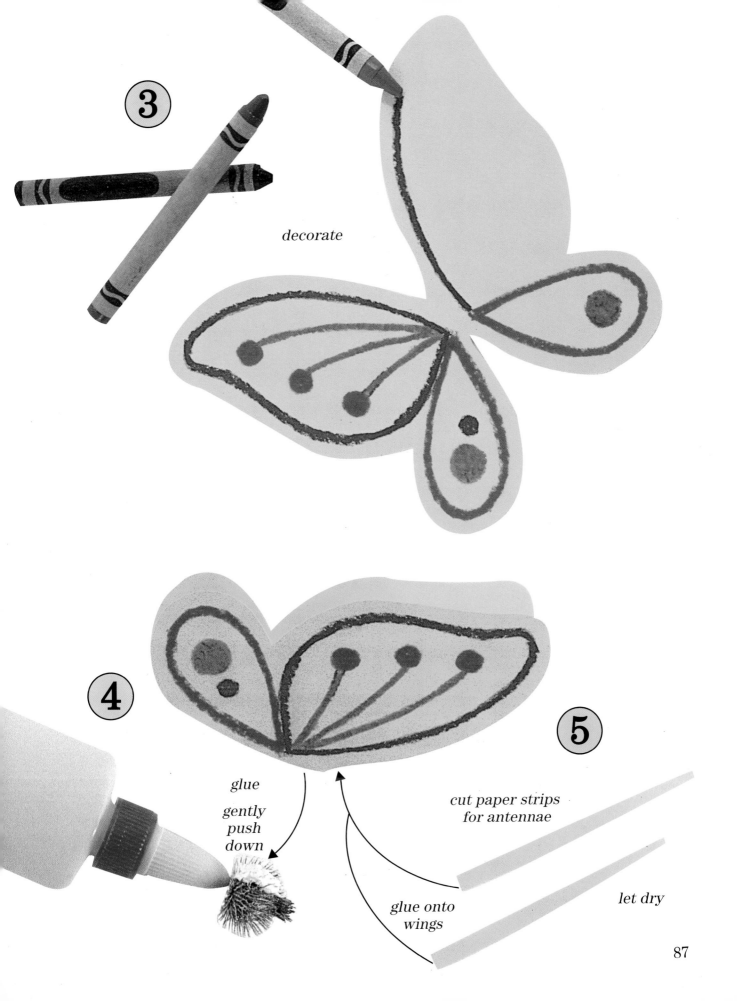

③

decorate

④

glue

gently
push
down

glue onto
wings

⑤

cut paper strips
for antennae

let dry

CORNHUSK DOLLS

- cornhusks and silk from raw ear of corn
- yarn
- scissors
- acrylic paint
- paintbrush

GREEN GIRL & BOY

1 save corn silk

pull husks off ear of corn

2

trim thick bottoms off husks

3

layer 3 husks

place corn silk across middle

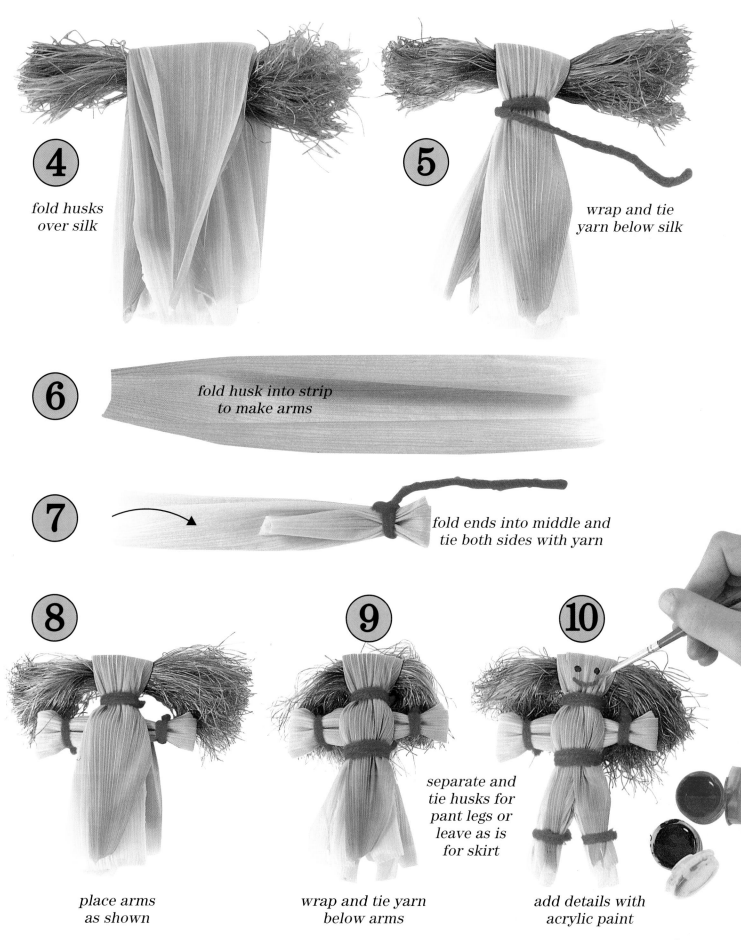

(4) fold husks
over silk

(5) wrap and tie
yarn below silk

(6) fold husk into strip
to make arms

(7) fold ends into middle and
tie both sides with yarn

(8) place arms
as shown

(9) wrap and tie yarn
below arms

(10) separate and
tie husks for
pant legs or
leave as is
for skirt

add details with
acrylic paint

89

DRIED DUO

- cornhusk dolls
- tempera paint
- water
- paintbrush
- scissors
- fabric
- yarn

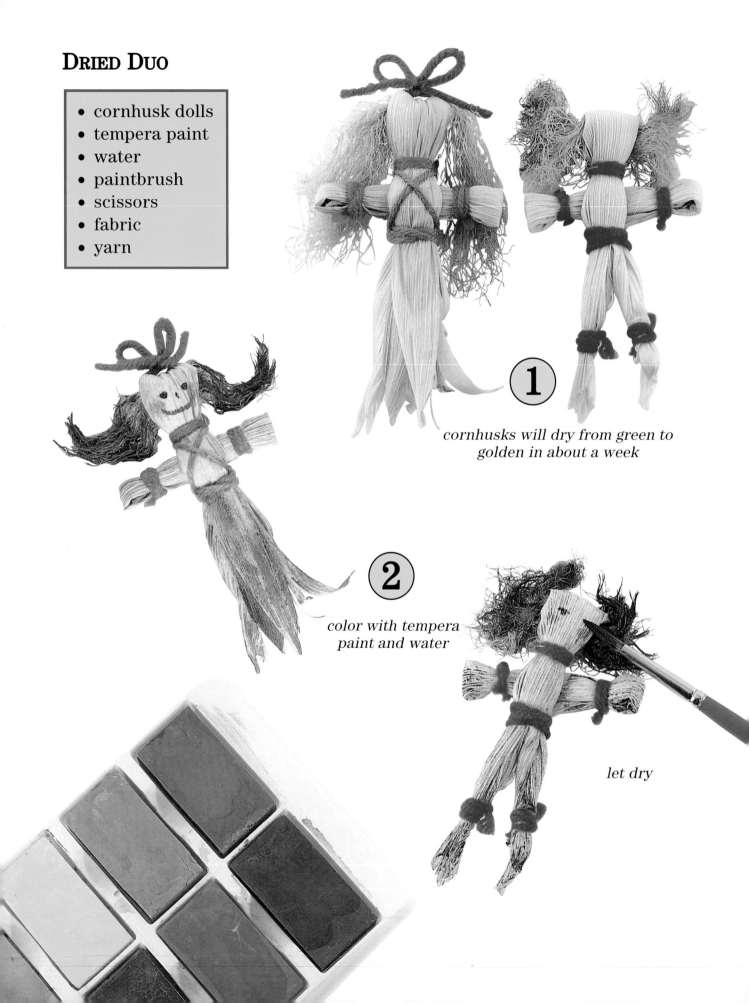

1 cornhusks will dry from green to golden in about a week

2 color with tempera paint and water

let dry

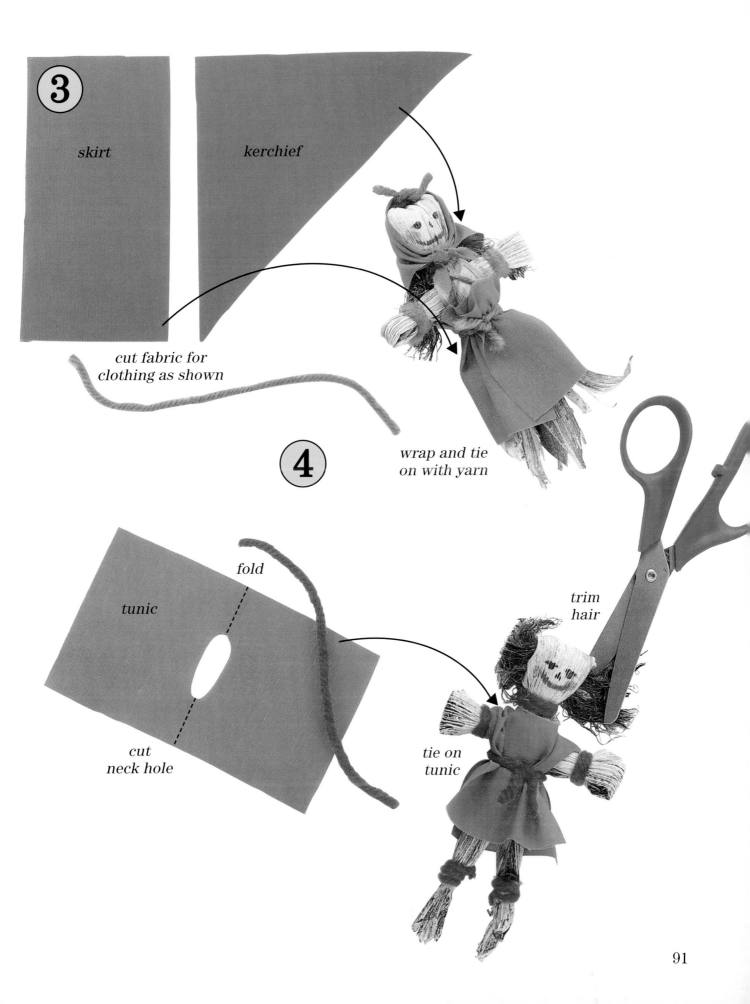

③

skirt

kerchief

cut fabric for
clothing as shown

wrap and tie
on with yarn

④

tunic

fold

cut
neck hole

trim
hair

tie on
tunic

91

MOSS GARDEN

- several spoonfuls of moss
- potting soil
- shallow dish
- twigs
- stones
- shells
- water
- *decorate as you like*

1 *collect moss from damp places among trees or along roadsides*

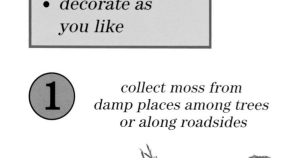

2 *fill shallow dish with potting soil*

3 *shape soil into valleys and hills*

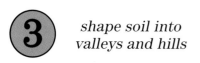

4 *make holes and dents in soil*

press in moss chunks

92

For Nutty Buddy, see p. 78.

5

push in twigs

add rocks and shells
to cover all soil

water lightly twice a week and
keep away from direct sunlight

93

FOREST FOLK

- twigs
- leaves and grass
- pine needles
- yarn
- scissors
- play clay
- acrylic paint and brush
- *decorate as you like*

TWIGGY

1

fold grass in half

2

wrap and tie grass with yarn

wrap and tie leaves

3

add details in acrylic paint

push into a ball of play clay to stand

Punk

1

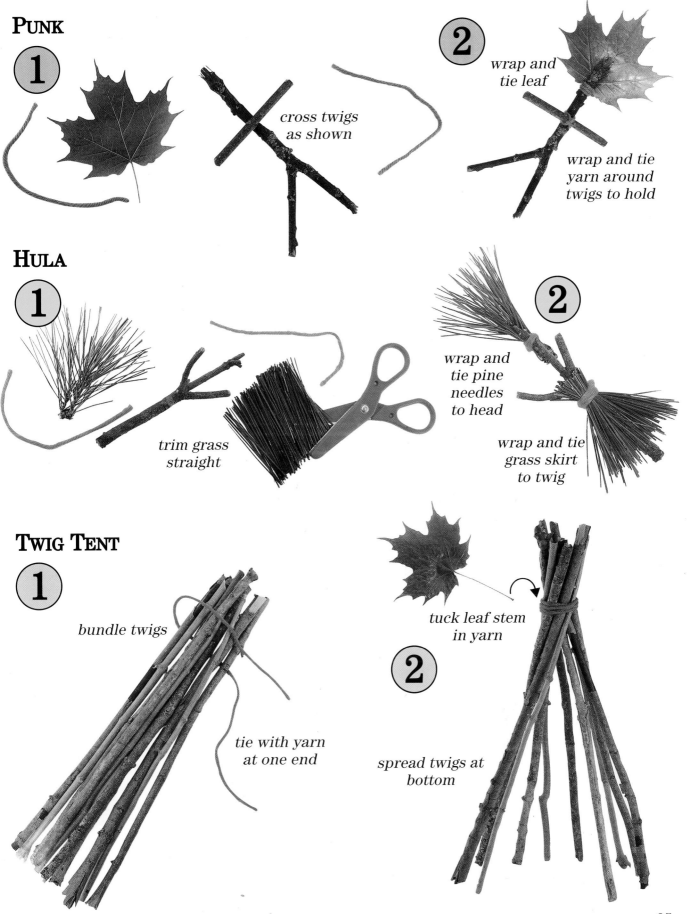

cross twigs
as shown

2

wrap and
tie leaf

wrap and tie
yarn around
twigs to hold

Hula

1

trim grass
straight

2

wrap and
tie pine
needles
to head

wrap and tie
grass skirt
to twig

Twig Tent

1

bundle twigs

tie with yarn
at one end

2

tuck leaf stem
in yarn

spread twigs at
bottom

TREASURE TRUNK

- egg carton
- acrylic paint and brush
- cardboard
- scissors
- 3 spoonfuls fine sand
- 3 small containers
- food color
- white glue

1

paint egg carton
with acrylic paint

let dry

3 put one spoonful
of sand in each
container

2

cut cardboard
to fit top of
carton

4

mix food color
into sand

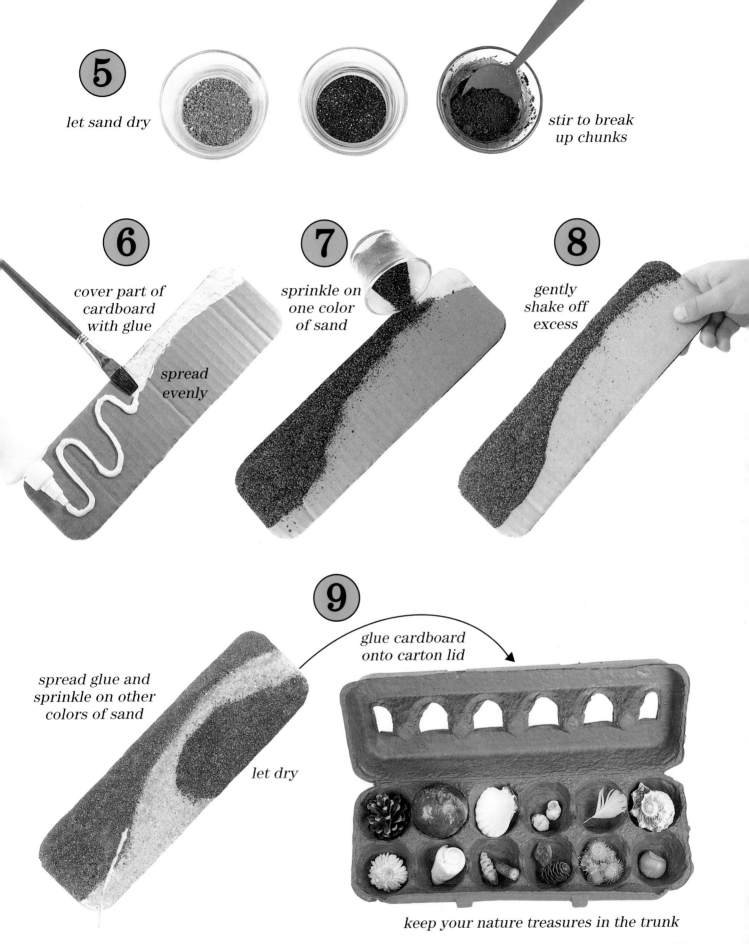

5 let sand dry

stir to break up chunks

6 cover part of cardboard with glue

spread evenly

7 sprinkle on one color of sand

8 gently shake off excess

9 glue cardboard onto carton lid

spread glue and sprinkle on other colors of sand

let dry

keep your nature treasures in the trunk

RESPECTING NATURE

- Before collecting grass, moss, leaves, flowers or twigs, ask a grown-up to make sure they are not harmful.
- Don't eat wild berries unless a grown-up tells you they are not poisonous.
- Pick only small amounts of growing things. Pick only what you need.
- Don't pull a plant up by its roots.

- Never take all the leaves, flowers or seeds from a plant.
- If there are only a few plants of one kind growing, leave them alone.
- Sometimes it's better to just look, not pick . . . and take the memory home.

Toys

LET'S MAKE TOYS

Are you ready to play? The following pages are filled with ideas and instructions for all kinds of toys that you can make yourself. These pages show what was used to make the toys in this chapter. Use your own imagination to find other things to use too. Don't forget to get permission to use anything you find at home.

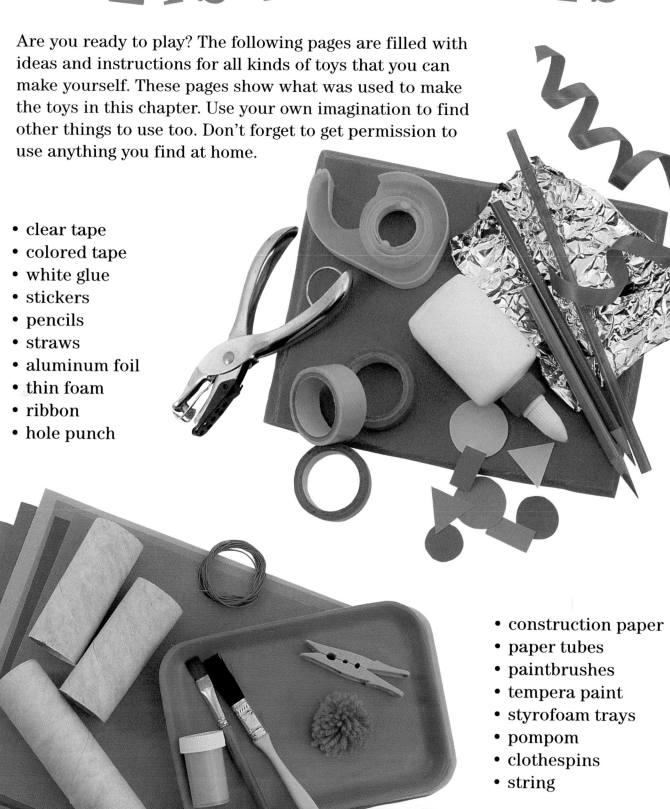

- clear tape
- colored tape
- white glue
- stickers
- pencils
- straws
- aluminum foil
- thin foam
- ribbon
- hole punch

- construction paper
- paper tubes
- paintbrushes
- tempera paint
- styrofoam trays
- pompom
- clothespins
- string

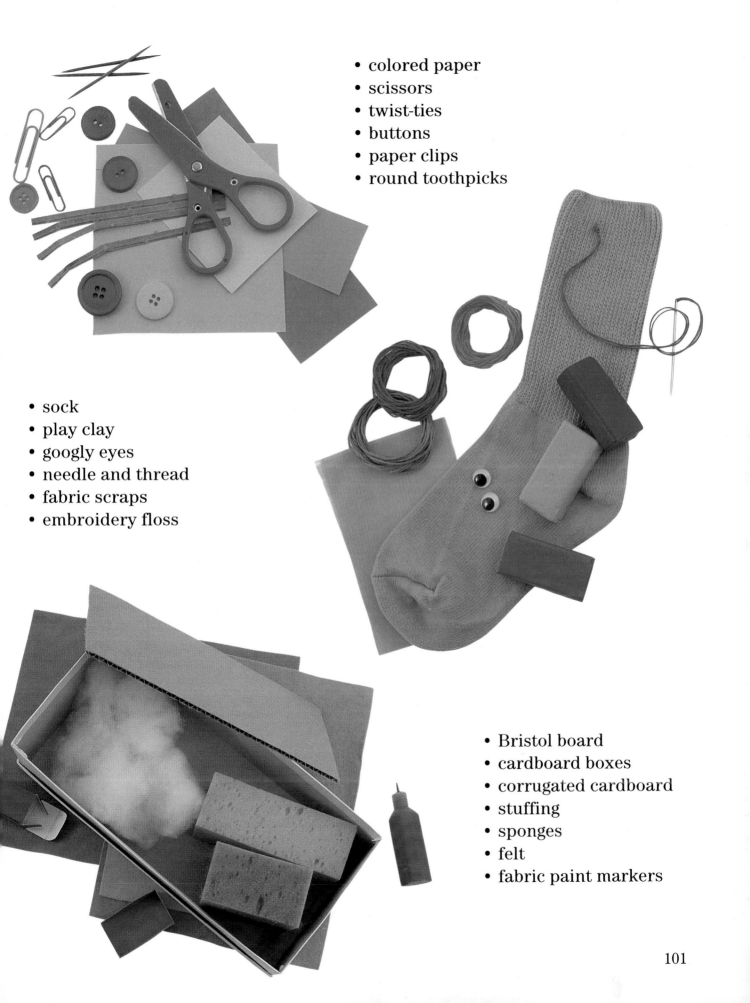

- colored paper
- scissors
- twist-ties
- buttons
- paper clips
- round toothpicks

- sock
- play clay
- googly eyes
- needle and thread
- fabric scraps
- embroidery floss

- Bristol board
- cardboard boxes
- corrugated cardboard
- stuffing
- sponges
- felt
- fabric paint markers

DECORATING TIPS

Hints for Kids and Parents

Use lots of color to make your toys bright. Before you begin, cover your table with newspaper or plastic to catch any drips.

TEMPERA PAINT is inexpensive and easy to use.
- use it on paper, cardboard and wood
  - wash it out with water
  - mix in a few drops of liquid soap to make the paint stick to a waxy surface
  - to keep it from rubbing off, make a finish with white glue (see below)

WHITE GLUE is safe and cleans up easily.
- use it to stick on colored paper and other decorations
- get the kind that dries clear
- let dry for 24 hours before playing
- make a mixture of ½ white glue and ½ water and brush over dried paint for a glossy, smear-proof finish

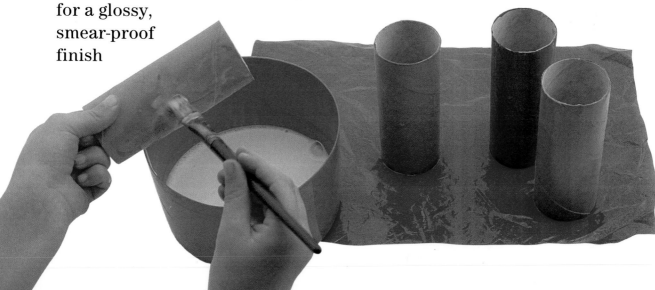

ACRYLIC PAINT or fabric paint comes in bright colors, and is waterproof once it dries.
- use it on almost any surface
- clean up with water while paint is still wet
- clean up fast — does NOT wash out of brushes, clothing or rugs when dry
- use a toothpick or fabric paint markers for small details

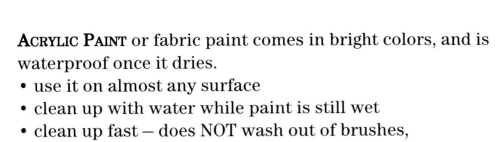
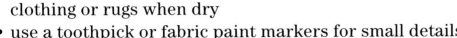

MARKERS AND CRAYONS are an inexpensive way to add color.
- use them to add details
- use mostly for small sections — might smudge if used to cover large pieces

COLORED TAPE AND STICKERS are easy to use, and they don't make any mess.

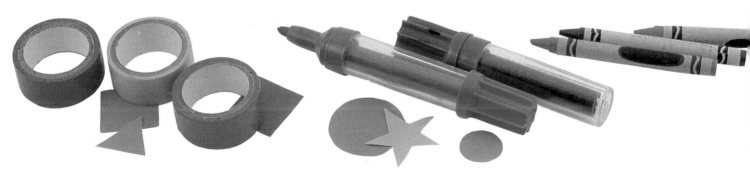

These are some of the ways the toys in this book have been decorated. And your toys can be even more special if you use ideas of your own. Be silly. Be daring. Be creative. Have fun!

FLYING FLAPPER

- construction paper
- pencil
- scissors
- stickers
- straw
- colored tape
- 4 to 6 m (about 13 to 20 feet) heavy thread
- *decorate as you like*

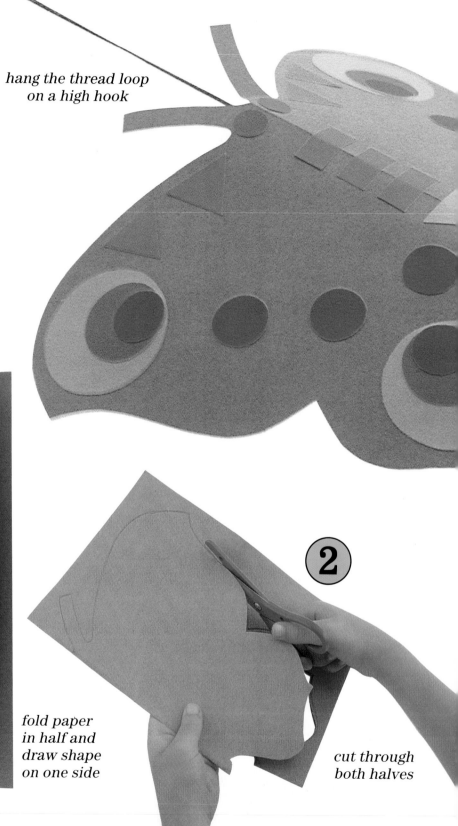

hang the thread loop on a high hook

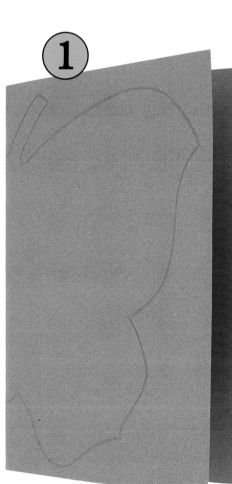

①

②

fold paper in half and draw shape on one side

cut through both halves

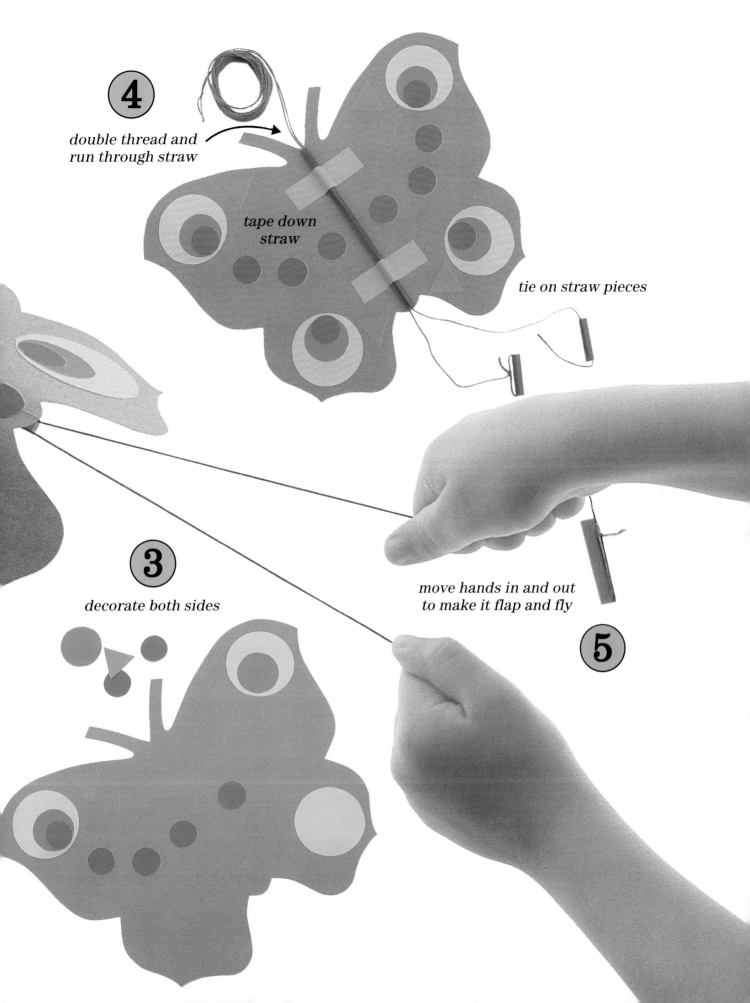

4

double thread and
run through straw

tape down
straw

tie on straw pieces

3

decorate both sides

move hands in and out
to make it flap and fly

5

TOY TRAIN

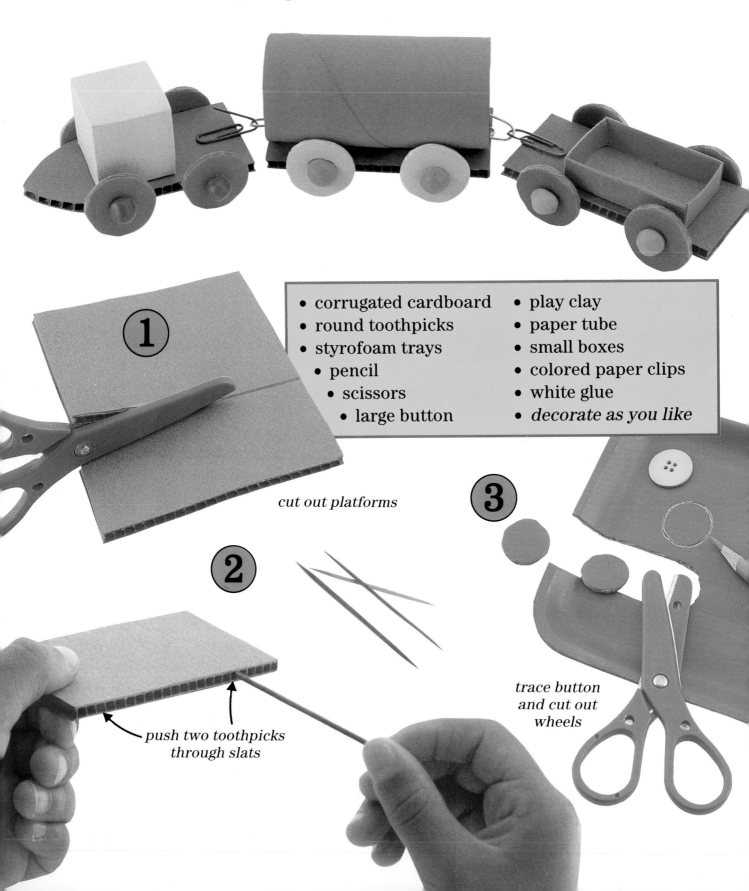

①

- corrugated cardboard
- round toothpicks
- styrofoam trays
- pencil
- scissors
- large button

- play clay
- paper tube
- small boxes
- colored paper clips
- white glue
- *decorate as you like*

cut out platforms

②

push two toothpicks through slats

③

trace button and cut out wheels

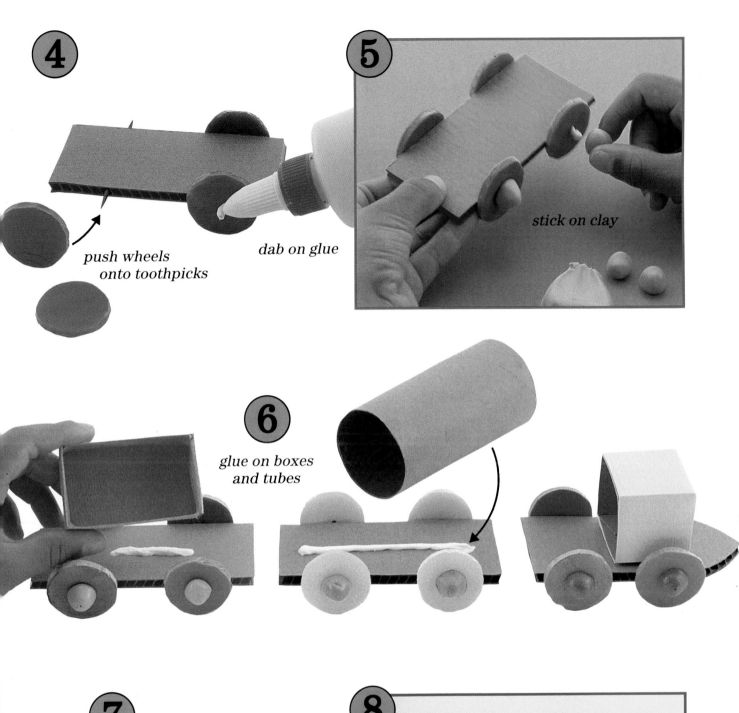

4

push wheels
onto toothpicks

dab on glue

5

stick on clay

6

glue on boxes
and tubes

7

glue on paper clip couplings

8

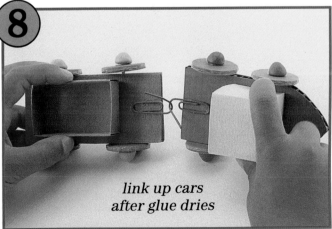

link up cars
after glue dries

JET GLIDER

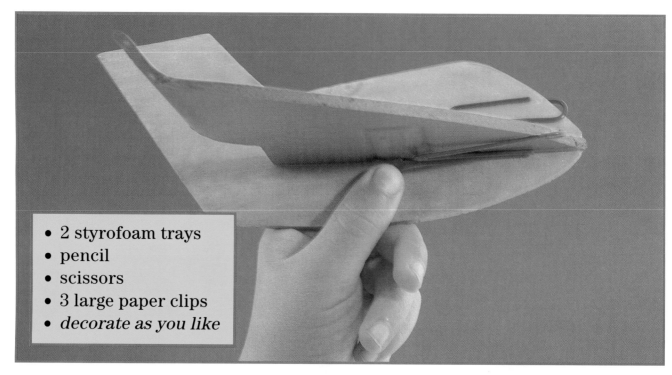

- 2 styrofoam trays
- pencil
- scissors
- 3 large paper clips
- *decorate as you like*

1

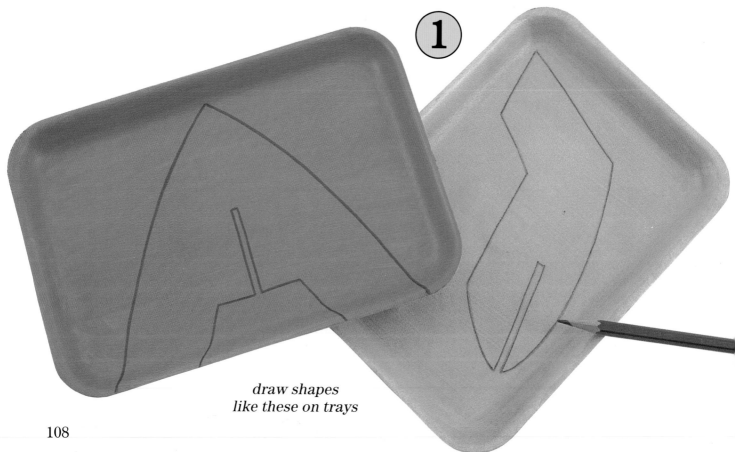

*draw shapes
like these on trays*

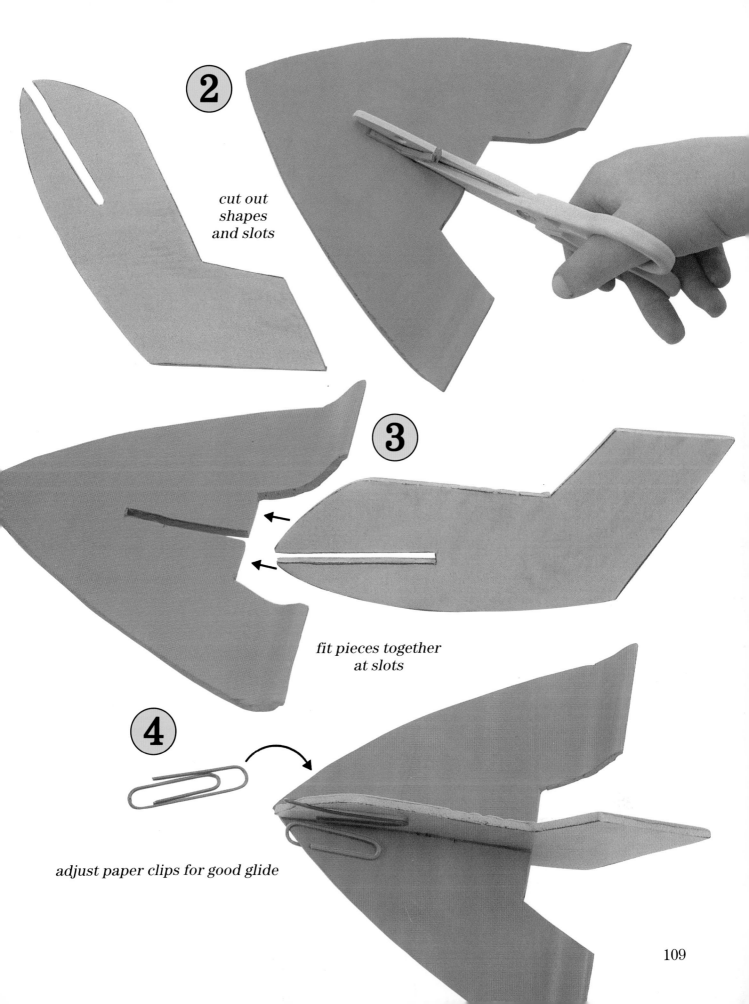

②

*cut out
shapes
and slots*

③

*fit pieces together
at slots*

④

adjust paper clips for good glide

RACE CAR

- clothespins (plastic or wood)
- buttons
- twist-ties
- straws
- scissors
- white glue
- colored tape
- *decorate as you like*

1 *thread a long twist-tie through button*

2 *twist and put through piece of straw*

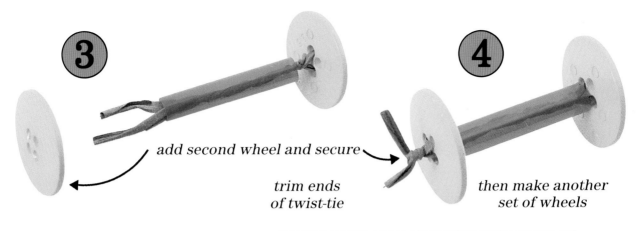

3

add second wheel and secure

trim ends
of twist-tie

4

then make another
set of wheels

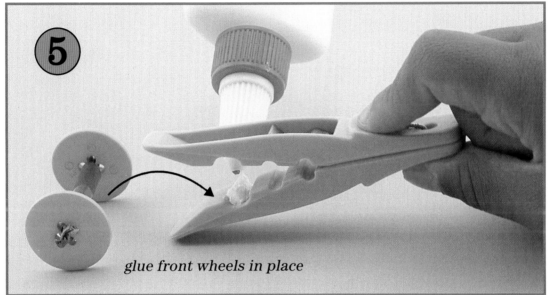

5

glue front wheels in place

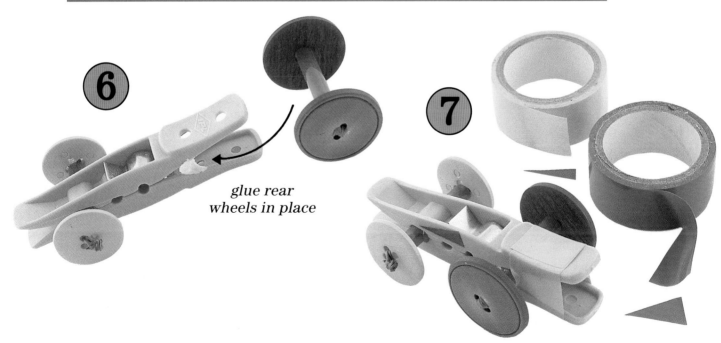

6

glue rear
wheels in place

7

wrap tape behind rear
wheels for durability

To make a race car ramp for your cars, see page 123.

BUNNY BUDDY

- *adult to help with sewing*
- sock
- stuffing
- scissors
- strong thread
- large needle
- yarn
- button
- googly eyes
- ribbon
- pompom

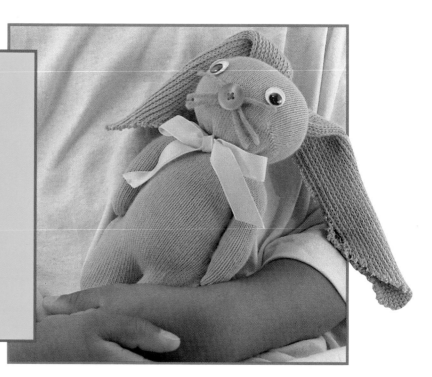

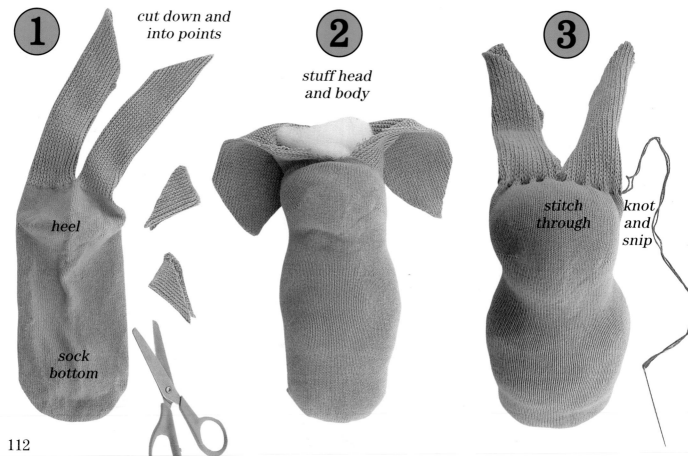

1 cut down and into points

heel

sock bottom

2 stuff head and body

3 stitch through

knot and snip

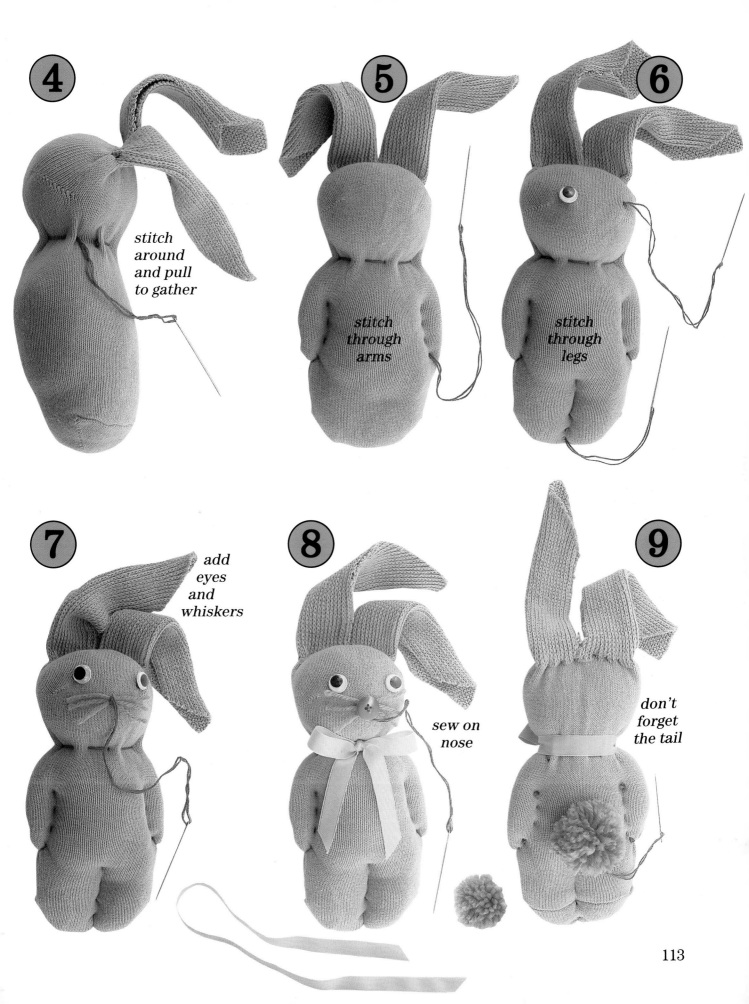

4 stitch around and pull to gather

5 stitch through arms

6 stitch through legs

7 add eyes and whiskers

8 sew on nose

9 don't forget the tail

EENSY WEENSY PEOPLE

- extra-long twist-ties
- embroidery floss
- scissors
- white glue
- acrylic paint
- *decorate as you like*

① ②

cut twist-tie in half for arms

bend another twist-tie for body

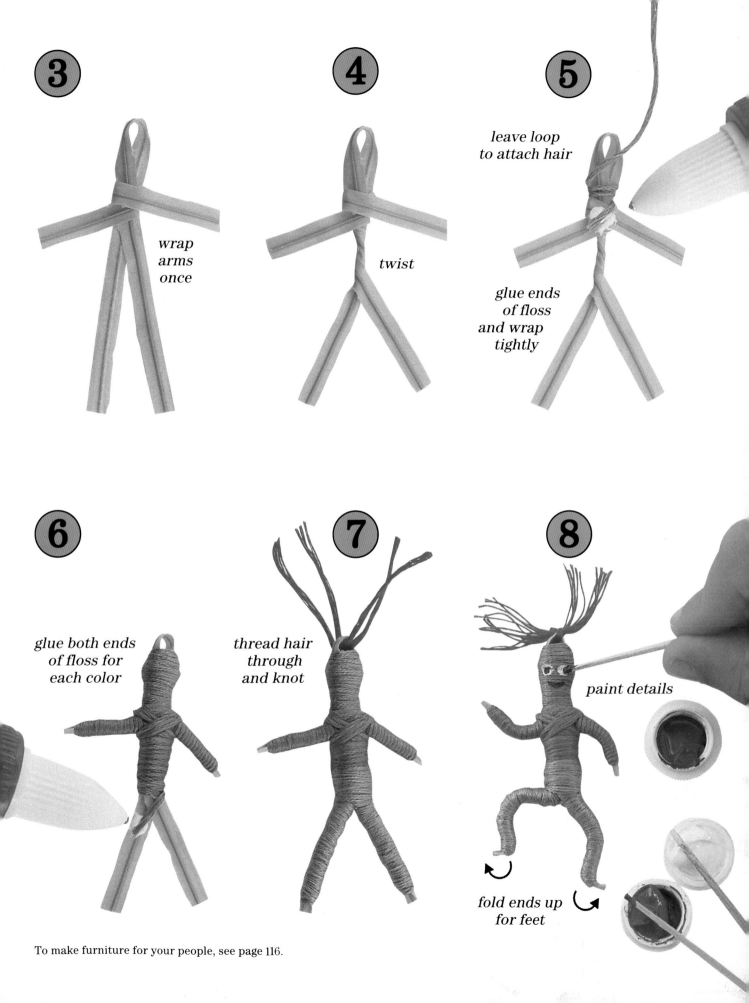

3 wrap arms once

4 twist

5 leave loop to attach hair

glue ends of floss and wrap tightly

6 glue both ends of floss for each color

7 thread hair through and knot

8 paint details

fold ends up for feet

To make furniture for your people, see page 116.

TOY FURNITURE

- sponges
- colored felt
- aluminum foil
- white glue
- scissors
- *decorate as you like*

CHAIR

①

②

BED

glue

glue

116

To make a house for your furniture, see page 118.

VANITY

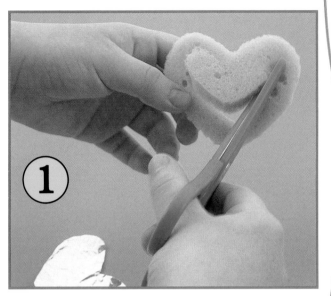

①

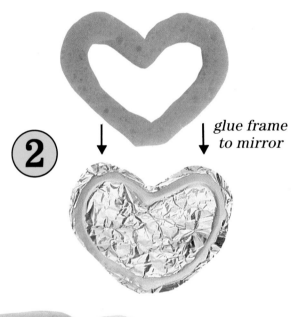

②

glue frame
to mirror

③ glue

CRADLE

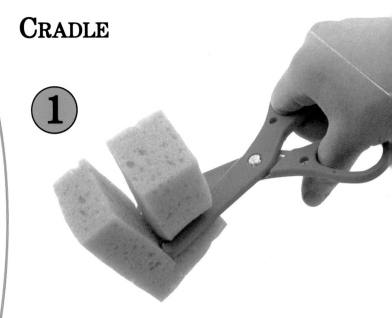

①

②

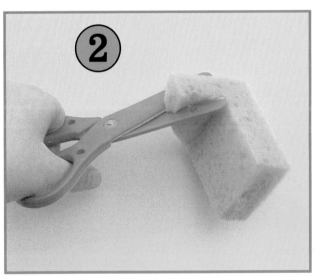

trim into
rounded
shape

③

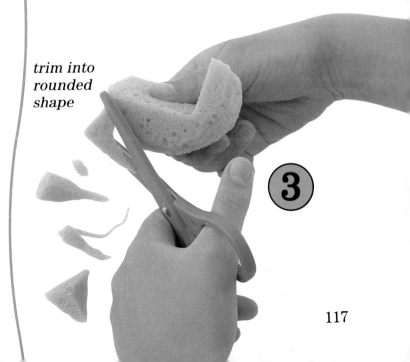

117

TOY HOUSE

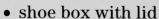

- shoe box with lid
- pencil
- scissors
- Bristol board
- colored paper
- paints and brush
- straw
- fabric scraps
- small boxes
- clear tape
- white glue
- *decorate as you like*

①

poke holes to start cutting windows and door

fold back

cut off flap

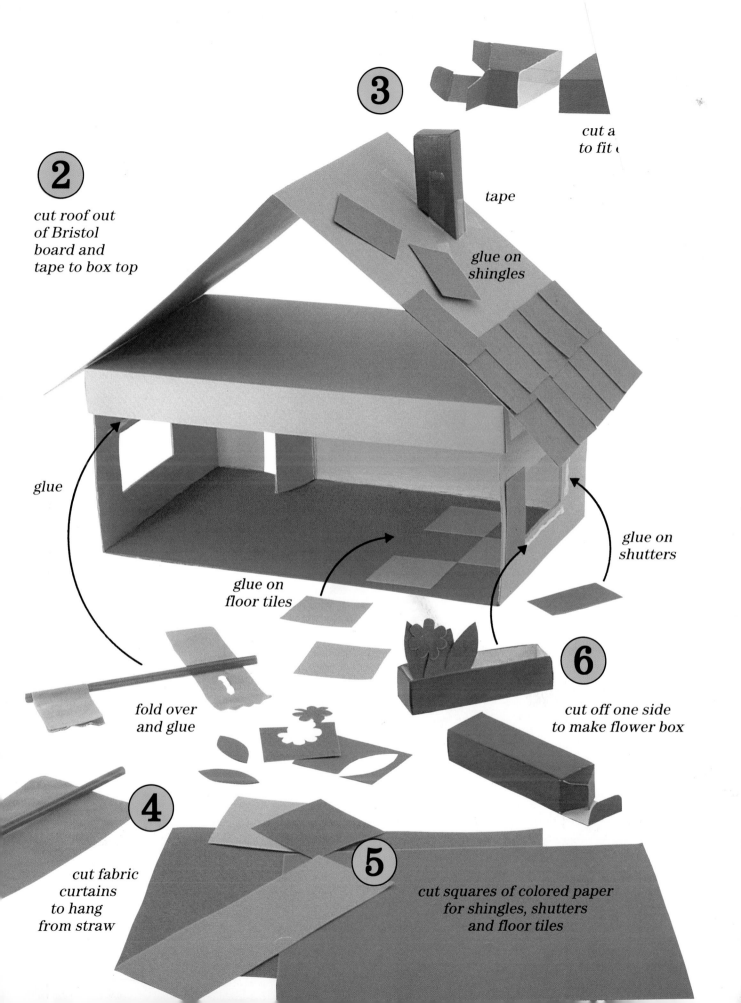

3

cut a
to fit

tape

2

cut roof out
of Bristol
board and
tape to box top

glue on
shingles

glue

glue on
floor tiles

glue on
shutters

6

fold over
and glue

cut off one side
to make flower box

4

cut fabric
curtains
to hang
from straw

5

cut squares of colored paper
for shingles, shutters
and floor tiles

DINOSAUR PUZZLE

- tracing paper
- markers
- scissors
- thin foam
- Bristol board
- acrylic/fabric paint
- white glue

*trace
the frame
and shapes
from this pattern
or make your own*

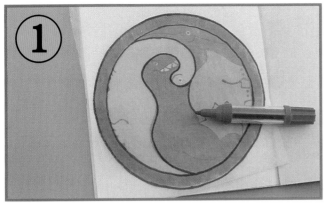
trace shapes and frame onto tracing paper

cut out paper shapes and frame

trace frame onto foam

trace rest of shapes onto foam

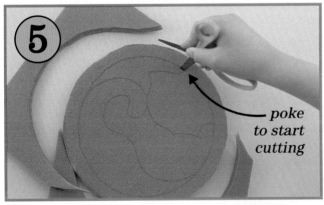
poke to start cutting

cut shapes out of foam

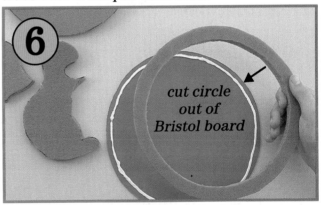
cut circle out of Bristol board

glue frame to Bristol board circle

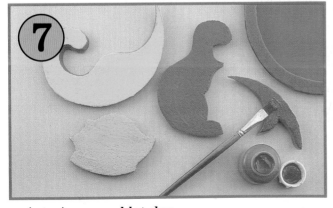
paint pieces and let dry

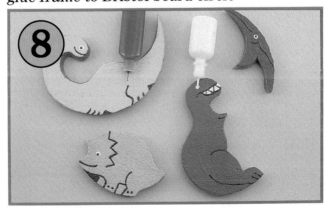
paint details

BUILD-A-TOY SET

- cardboard boxes
- colored construction paper
- paper towel tubes
- toilet paper tubes
- pencil
- scissors
- tempera paint
- white glue *(optional)*
- liquid soap *(optional)*

cut out circles, rectangles and triangles

decorate as you like

cut slits into opposite sides of each end of tube

Use white glue to keep paint from rubbing off; see page 102.
Use liquid soap to make paint stick to waxy surfaces; see page 102.

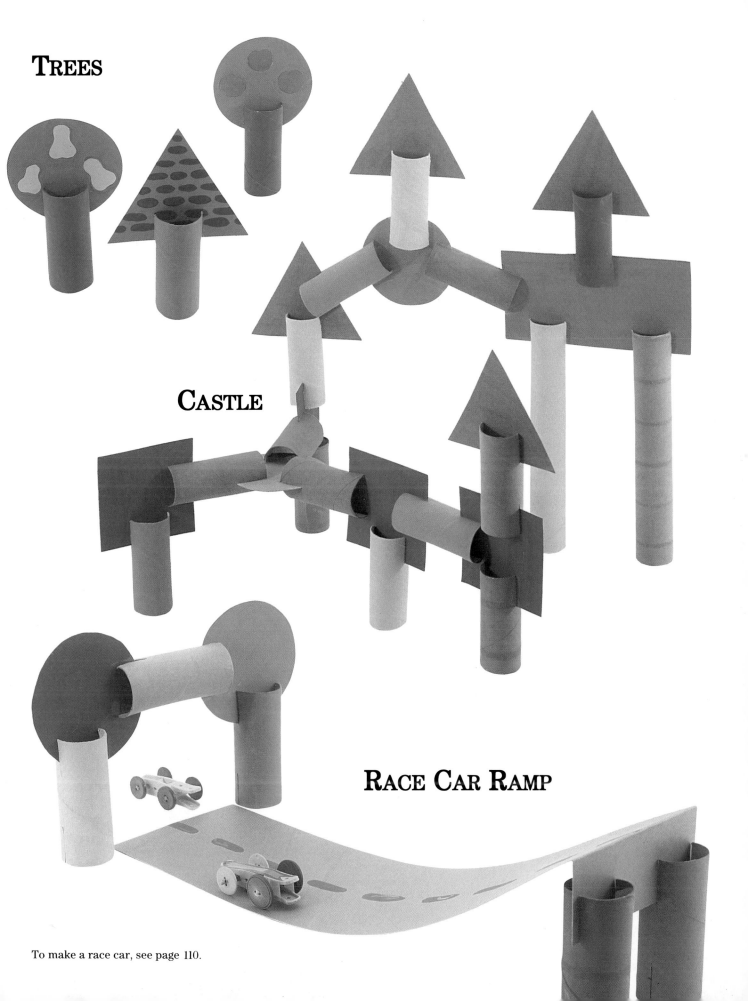

TREES

CASTLE

RACE CAR RAMP

To make a race car, see page 110.

Log Cabin

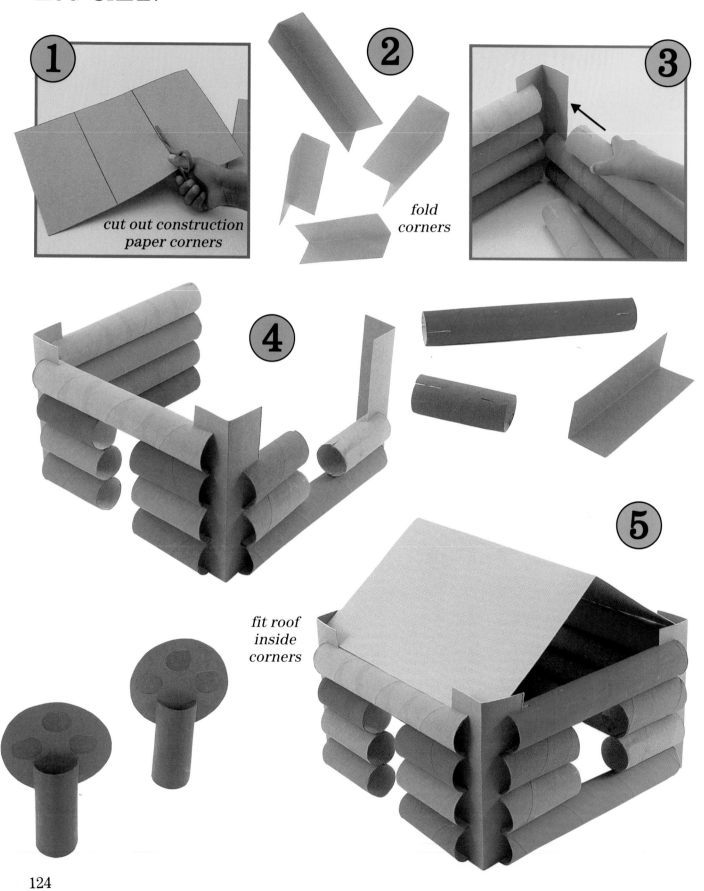

1 cut out construction paper corners

2 fold corners

3

4

5 fit roof inside corners

HORSE

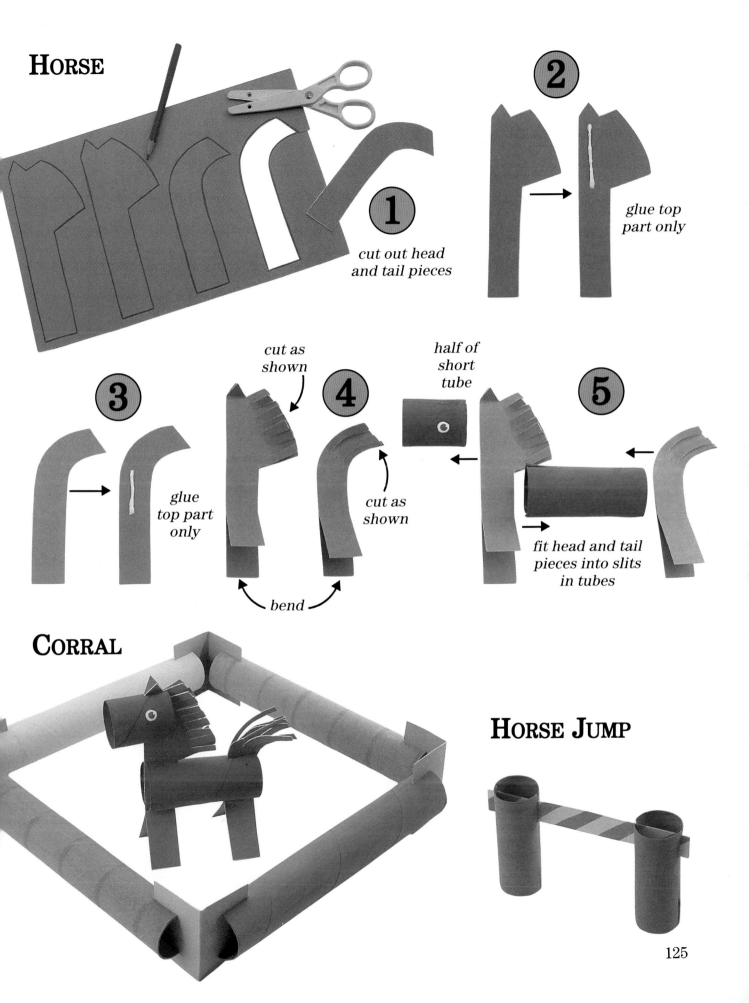

1 cut out head and tail pieces

2 glue top part only

3 glue top part only

cut as shown

4 cut as shown

bend

half of short tube

5 fit head and tail pieces into slits in tubes

CORRAL

HORSE JUMP

125

MY TOY BOX

- cardboard box with hinged lid
- colored paper
- white glue that dries clear
- water
- bowl
- pencil
- hole punch
- string
- large button

1

tear strips and pieces of colored paper

2

dip paper pieces into mixture and smooth onto box

½ white glue and ½ water

3

cover box and let dry overnight

punch holes on top and front of box near edge

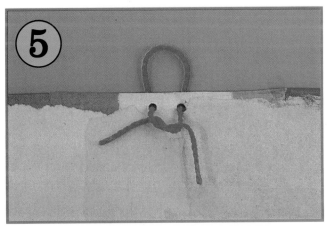

tie string to make loop on top of box lid

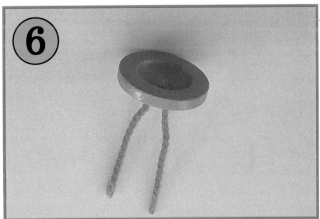

thread button on another piece of string

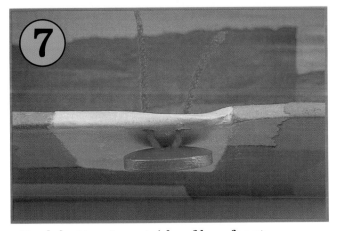

attach button to outside of box front

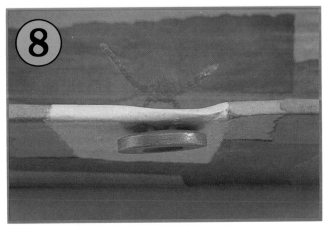

tie down button

To see the finished toy box, turn the page!

Games

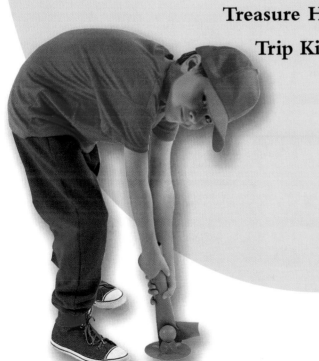

LET'S MAKE GAMES

These games are loads of fun—and they're easy to make, too. You'll see all the materials used for making the games in this chapter on these two pages of the book. You might also have your own ideas for using other things you can find around your home (always get permission to use what you find). To play some of the games, you'll need a place without things that might break, or younger children that could get hurt. Play safely and have fun!

- aluminum foil
- white glue
- yarn
- milk or juice carton
- funnel
- Bristol board
- balloons
- spoon
- flour or fine sand

- bowl
- plastic bag
- acrylic paint
- bendable straw
- paintbrush
- cardboard box
- paper bags
- egg carton
- soil

- small boxes
- sponge
- face cloth
- tape
- stapler
- cardboard
- light-weight chain
- beads
- star stickers
- foam tray
- plastic wrap
- markers

- construction paper
- tracing paper
- paper tubes
- masking tape
- hole punch
- rubber bands
- buttons
- bottle caps
- scissors
- paper clips

- envelopes
- soft lead pencil
- chalk
- pencil crayons
- die
- googly eyes
- toy shovel
- fabric marker
- candies
- shoe box
- felt

TANGLE

- 2 milk or juice cartons
- scissors
- masking tape
- six colors of construction paper
- pencil
- white glue

(1)

cut

cut two square
boxes from
carton bottoms

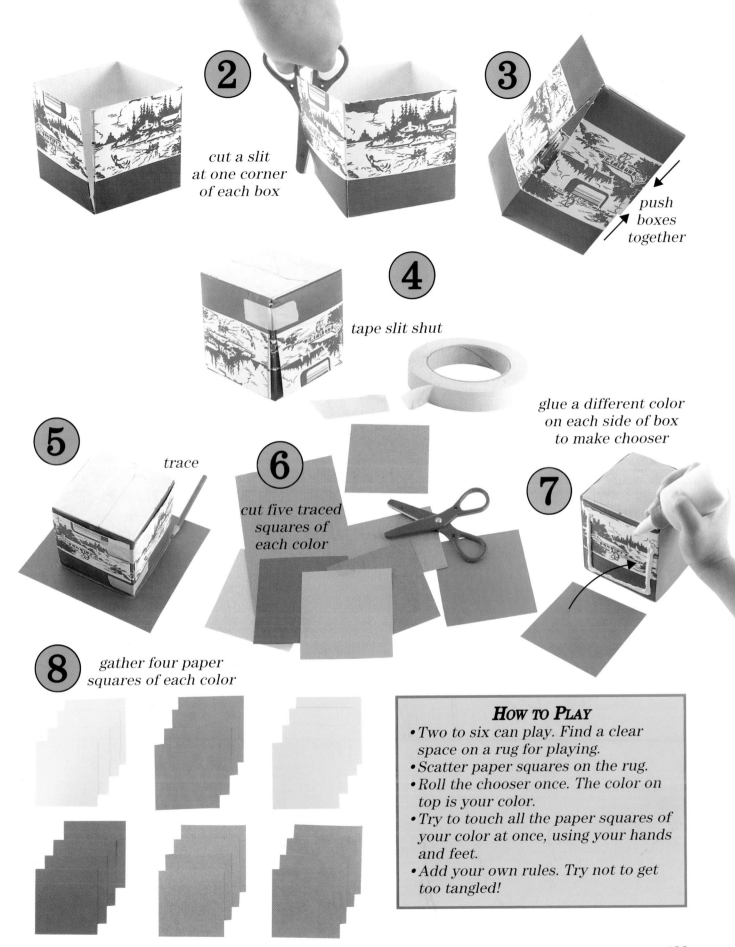

② cut a slit at one corner of each box

③ push boxes together

④ tape slit shut

⑤ trace

⑥ cut five traced squares of each color

glue a different color on each side of box to make chooser

⑦

⑧ gather four paper squares of each color

HOW TO PLAY
- Two to six can play. Find a clear space on a rug for playing.
- Scatter paper squares on the rug.
- Roll the chooser once. The color on top is your color.
- Try to touch all the paper squares of your color at once, using your hands and feet.
- Add your own rules. Try not to get too tangled!

133

HATCHING EGG

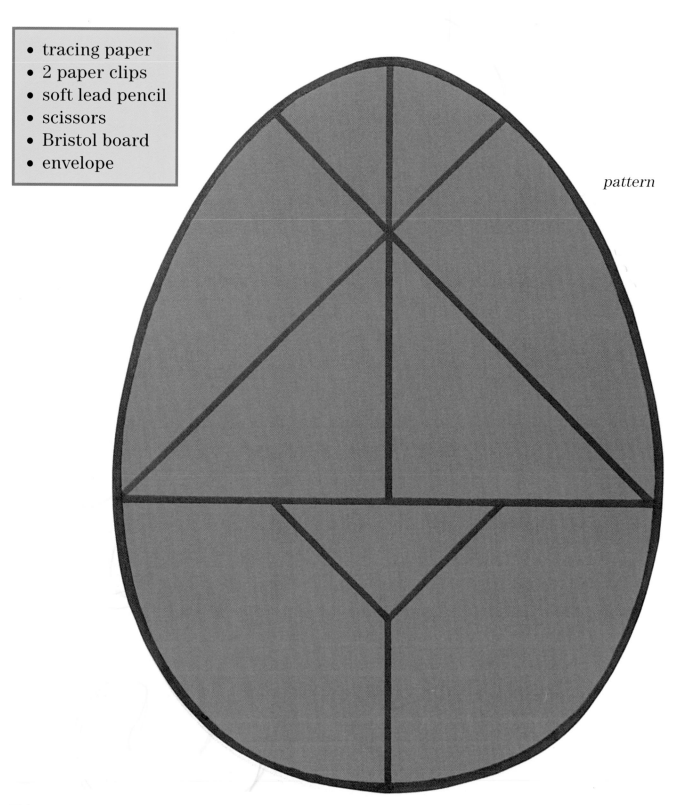

pattern

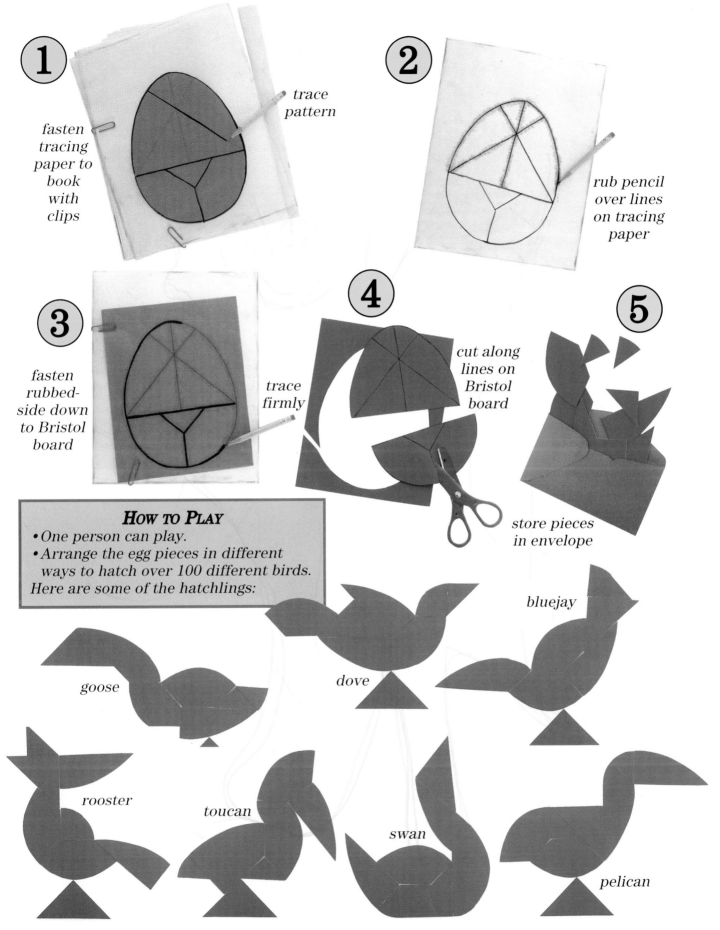

1 *fasten tracing paper to book with clips*

trace pattern

2 *rub pencil over lines on tracing paper*

3 *fasten rubbed-side down to Bristol board*

trace firmly

4 *cut along lines on Bristol board*

5 *store pieces in envelope*

HOW TO PLAY
• One person can play.
• Arrange the egg pieces in different ways to hatch over 100 different birds. Here are some of the hatchlings:

goose

dove

bluejay

rooster

toucan

swan

pelican

135

MONKEY RACE

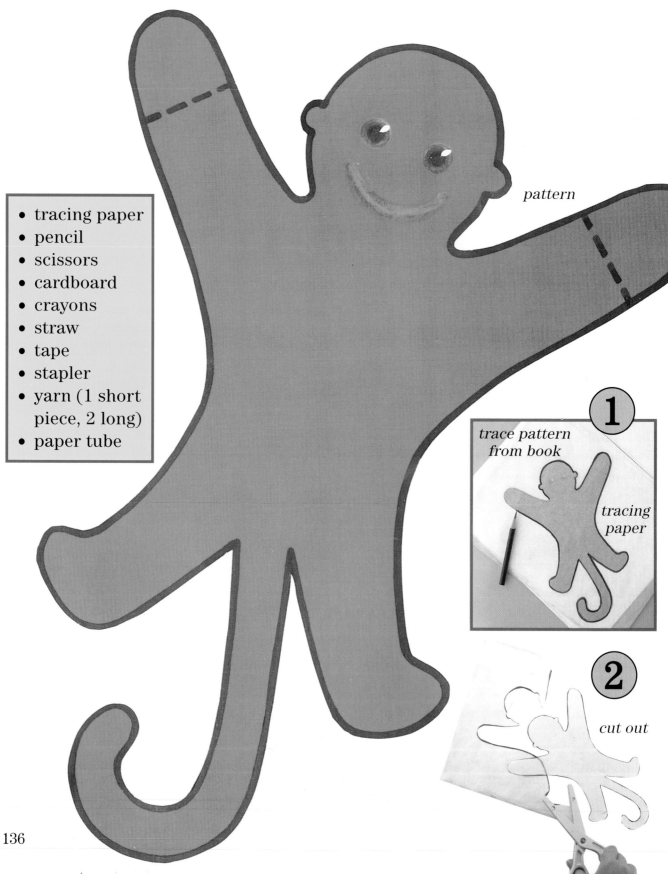

pattern

- tracing paper
- pencil
- scissors
- cardboard
- crayons
- straw
- tape
- stapler
- yarn (1 short piece, 2 long)
- paper tube

1 trace pattern from book

tracing paper

2 cut out

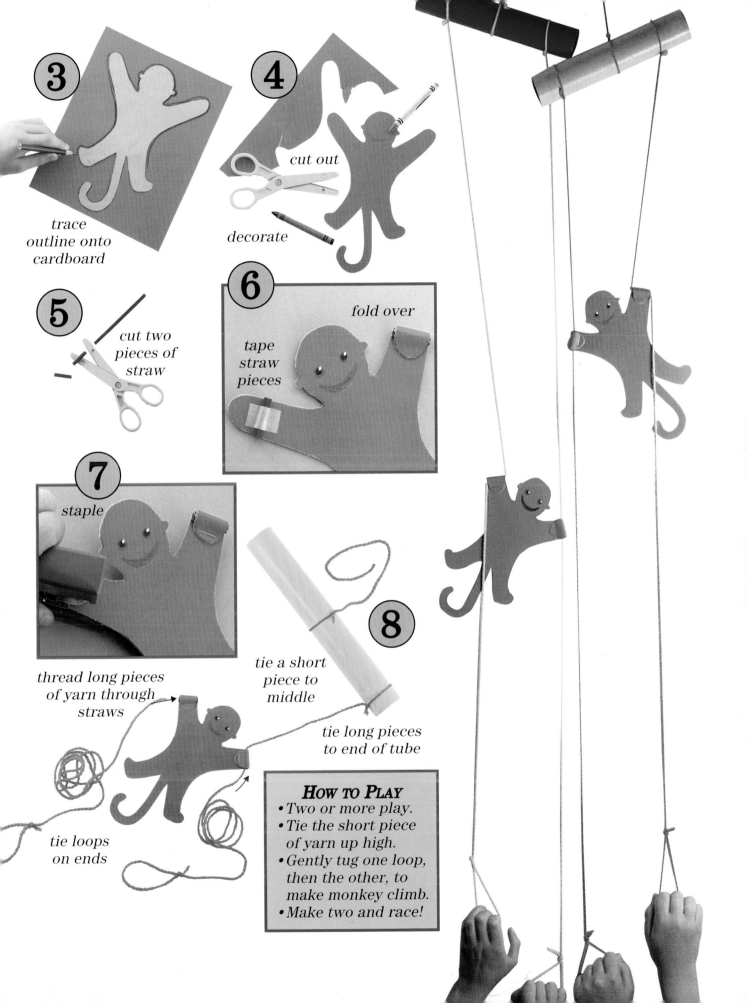

3 trace outline onto cardboard

4 cut out

decorate

5 cut two pieces of straw

6 tape straw pieces

fold over

7 staple

thread long pieces of yarn through straws

tie loops on ends

8 tie a short piece to middle

tie long pieces to end of tube

HOW TO PLAY
• Two or more play.
• Tie the short piece of yarn up high.
• Gently tug one loop, then the other, to make monkey climb.
• Make two and race!

SQUISHERS

- large balloons
- fine sand or flour
- funnel
- spoon
- pencil

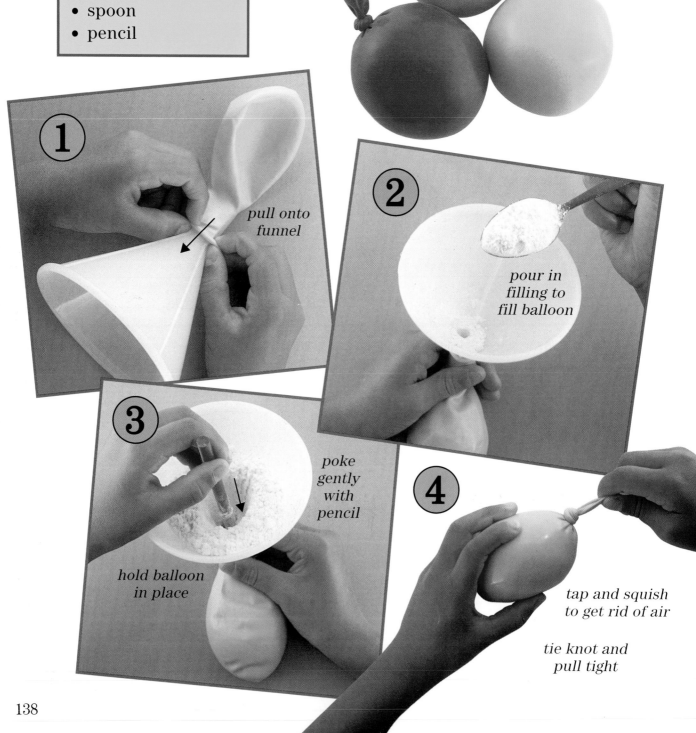

1 pull onto funnel

2 pour in filling to fill balloon

3 poke gently with pencil

hold balloon in place

4 tap and squish to get rid of air

tie knot and pull tight

138

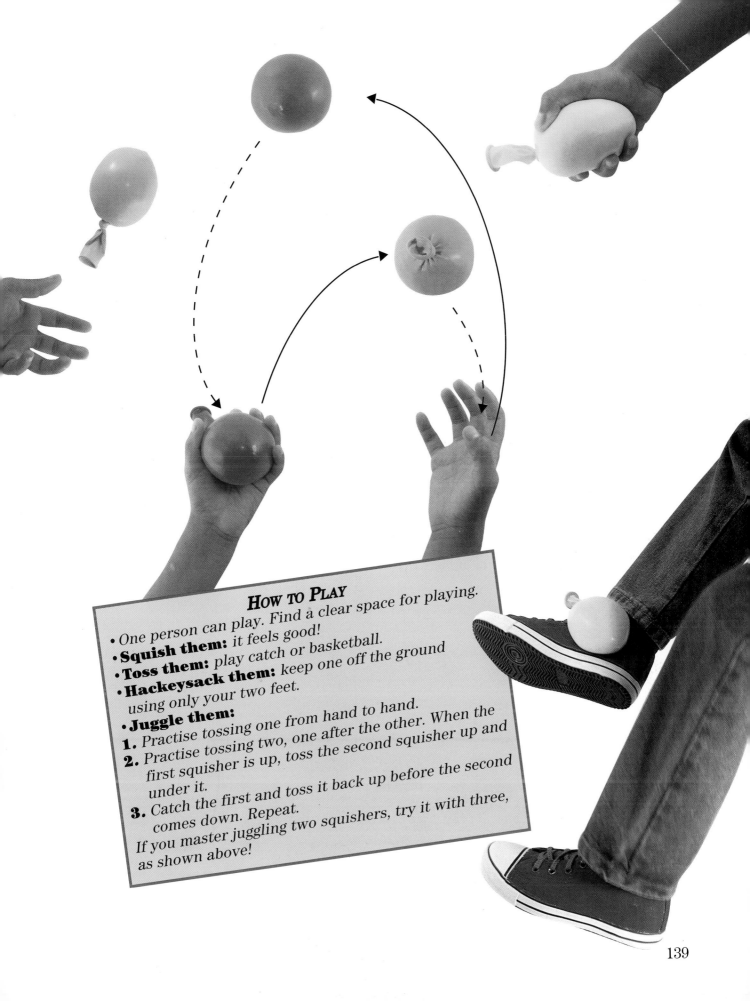

How to Play

- One person can play. Find a clear space for playing.
- **Squish them:** it feels good!
- **Toss them:** play catch or basketball.
- **Hackeysack them:** keep one off the ground using only your two feet.
- **Juggle them:**
  1. Practise tossing one from hand to hand.
  2. Practise tossing two, one after the other. When the first squisher is up, toss the second squisher up and under it.
  3. Catch the first and toss it back up before the second comes down. Repeat.

  If you master juggling two squishers, try it with three, as shown above!

CAT AND MOUSE

- yellow sponge
- scissors
- egg carton
- acrylic paint
- paintbrush
- white glue
- yarn
- 8 googly eyes
- construction paper
- small box
- markers
- 1 large piece of Bristol board
- 1 die

CHEESE

cut sponge into ten triangle-shaped pieces

MICE

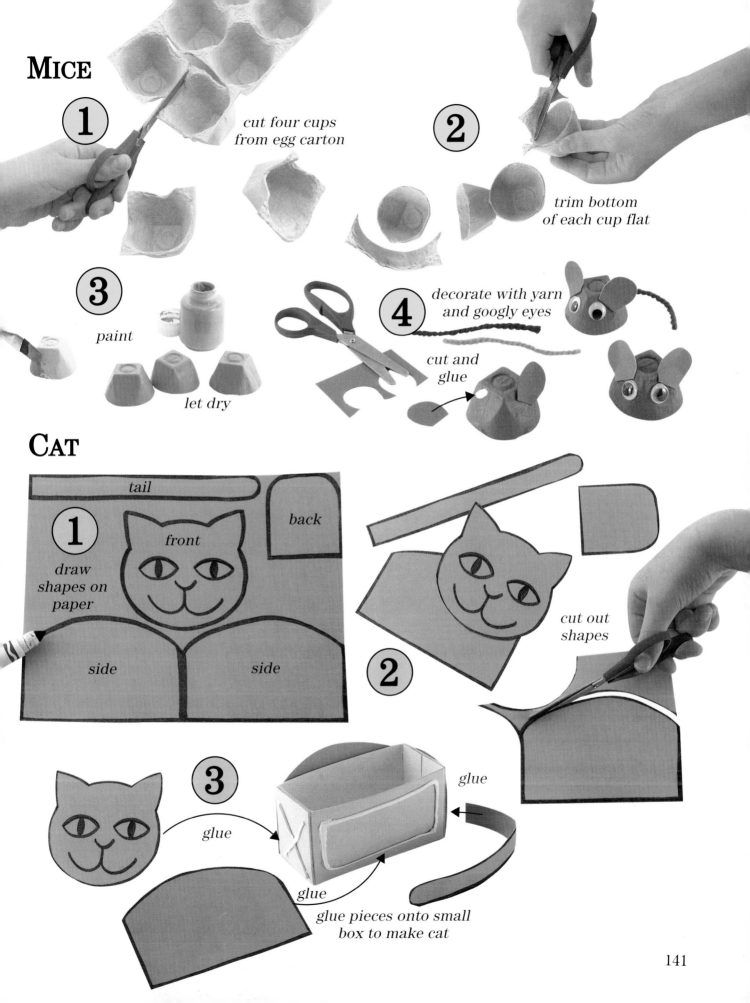

1 cut four cups from egg carton

2 trim bottom of each cup flat

3 paint

let dry

4 decorate with yarn and googly eyes

cut and glue

CAT

1 draw shapes on paper

tail

back

front

side   side

2 cut out shapes

3 glue

glue

glue

glue pieces onto small box to make cat

GAMEBOARD

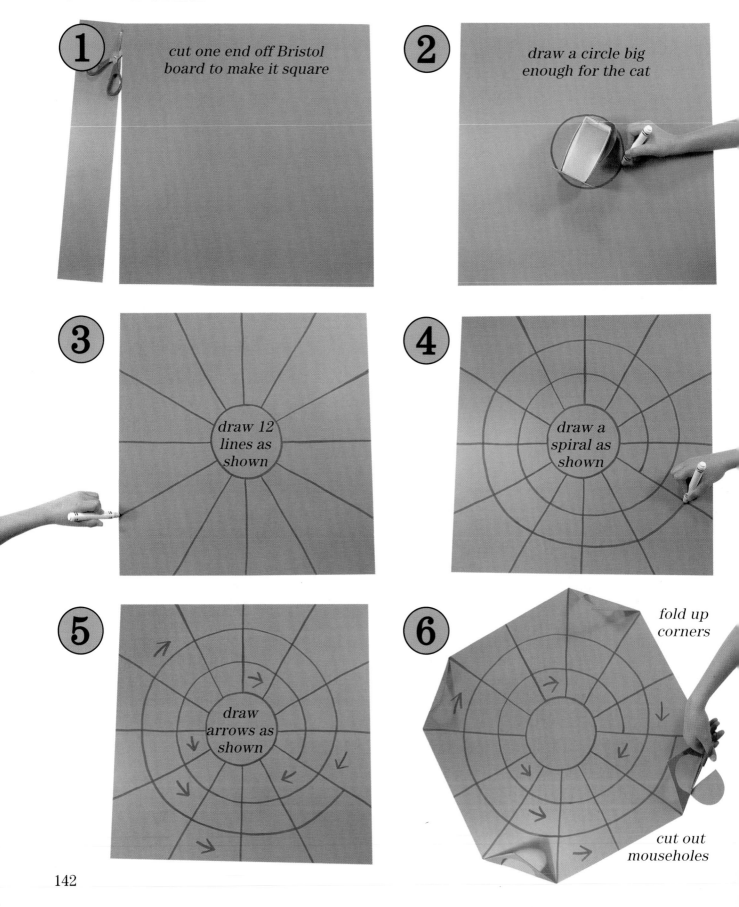

1 cut one end off Bristol board to make it square

2 draw a circle big enough for the cat

3 draw 12 lines as shown

4 draw a spiral as shown

5 draw arrows as shown

6 fold up corners

cut out mouseholes

142

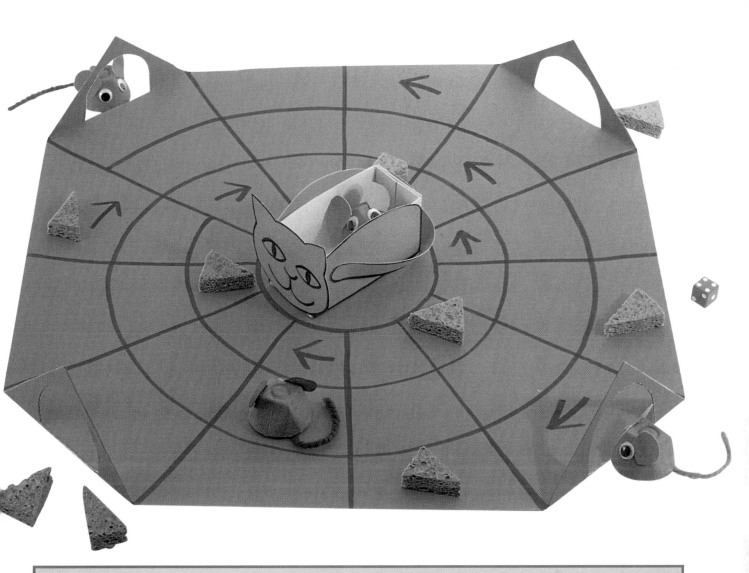

How to Play

- *Two or more play this cooperative game.*
- *Place the cat in the middle. Mice that land in the row of spaces directly in front of the cat are caught and go in the cat.*
- *Scatter cheese on the board. Mice start at the mouseholes.*
- *Take turns rolling the die. Choose any mouse and move along the spiral towards the center. If a mouse reaches the center, it turns around and returns to its hole.*
- *When your roll lands a mouse on the same square as a piece of cheese, the mouse picks up the cheese. The mice take the cheese, one piece at a time, back to the mouseholes. After a mouse gets a piece of cheese into a hole, it starts again. All moves are by roll of die.*
- *When your roll lands a mouse on an arrow, the cat turns one space in the direction of the arrow. Any mice now in the row of spaces directly in front of the cat are caught and go in the cat.*
- *Players plan together to outsmart the cat! Try to get as many mice with their pieces of cheese as you can safely back into the mouseholes.*

PIN BALL BOWL

- fat paper tube
- thin paper tube
- 5 short tubes
- acrylic paint
- paintbrush
- hole punch
- masking tape
- 2 rubber bands
- yarn
- aluminum foil

 ①

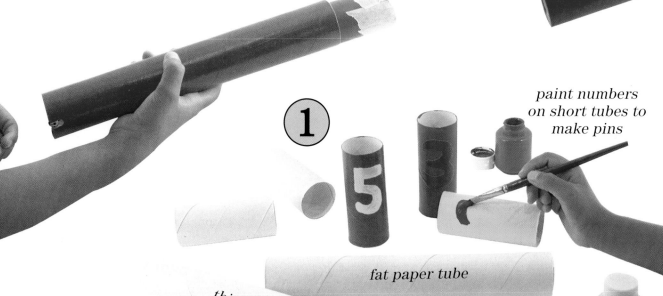

paint numbers on short tubes to make pins

fat paper tube

thin paper tube

②

punch holes as shown

fat paper tube

tape over end of thin tube

thin paper tube

3

attach rubber bands to fat tube

4

put thin tube inside

push rubber band ends through holes in thin tube

5

tie rubber bands together with yarn

6

crumple aluminum foil into balls

7

HOW TO PLAY
- Two or more play. Find a clear space for playing.
- Arrange pins in a "∨" shape. Load ball, pull back the inside tube and let go to shoot ball. Add up the points printed on the pins you've knocked down.
- The player with the most points wins.

OWL EYES

- *adult to help punch holes*
- small box
- paper
- pencil
- scissors
- white glue
- foam tray
- hole punch
- 6 beads
- plastic wrap
- tape

1
trace box onto paper

2 cut out
draw owls on paper

3 back
glue paper to tray

4 cut out

5 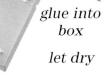 punch eye holes

6 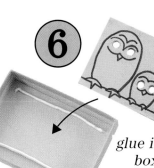 glue into box

let dry

7 put in beads

8 stretch wrap over box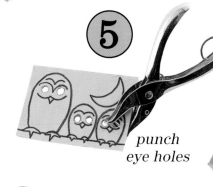

9 tape around edges of wrap

HOW TO PLAY
- One person can play.
- Shake box gently to roll beads into holes.

FEED THE SHARK

- Bristol board
- markers
- face cloth
- pencil
- light-weight chain
- tape

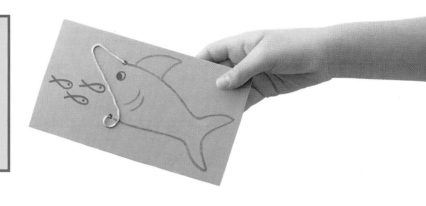

1 draw shark and fish

Bristol board

2 poke two holes with pencil as shown

folded face cloth

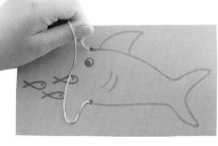

3 put chain ends through holes

4

back

adjust chain length then tape ends

HOW TO PLAY
- One person can play.
- Shake gently to open shark's mouth around fish.

SIX MAN MORRIS

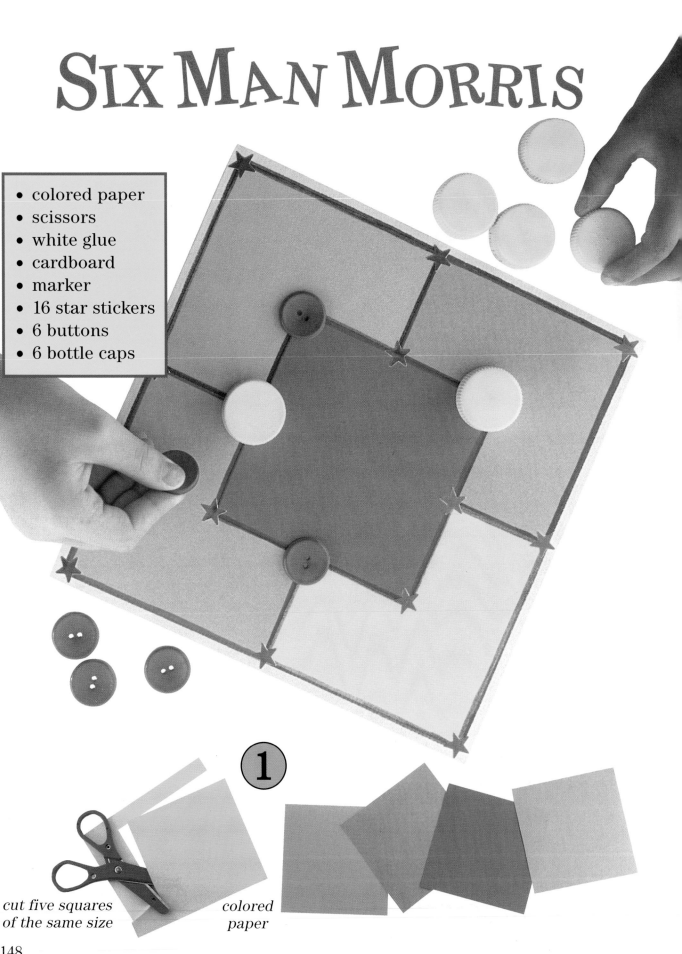

- colored paper
- scissors
- white glue
- cardboard
- marker
- 16 star stickers
- 6 buttons
- 6 bottle caps

①

cut five squares
of the same size

colored
paper

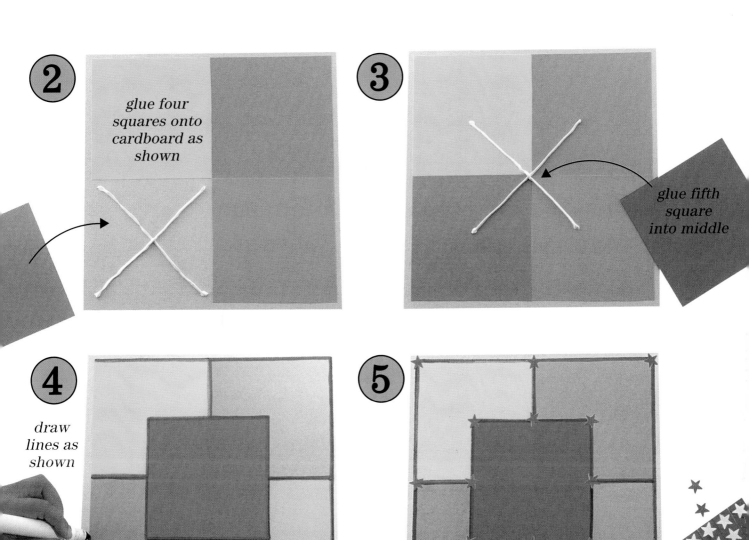

2 glue four squares onto cardboard as shown

3 glue fifth square into middle

4 draw lines as shown

marker

5 press on star stickers as shown

HOW TO PLAY

- Two people play. The best way to learn this game is to play it!
- Each player has either six buttons or six bottle caps as playing pieces.
- Start by placing your pieces on uncovered stars. Take turns placing one piece on the board at a time.
- Throughout the game, try to get three pieces in a row along a line. These will be "safe." Any time you get a safe row of three on the board, you can take one of the other player's pieces, as long as it is not in a safe row.

- When a piece is taken, it is out of play. Once all your pieces are on the board or out of play, take turns moving your remaining pieces, one at a time. A piece can move along any line to an uncovered star next to it. (You can't make the same row of three more than once.)
- When you have only three pieces left, you can jump to any uncovered star on the board.
- You win when the other player has only two pieces left, or if you have blocked all the other player's moves.

Mini Golf

Hazards

- 4 cardboard boxes
- pencil
- scissors
- Bristol board
- glue or tape
- acrylic paint and brush
- paper tube
- *decorate as you like*

Elephant

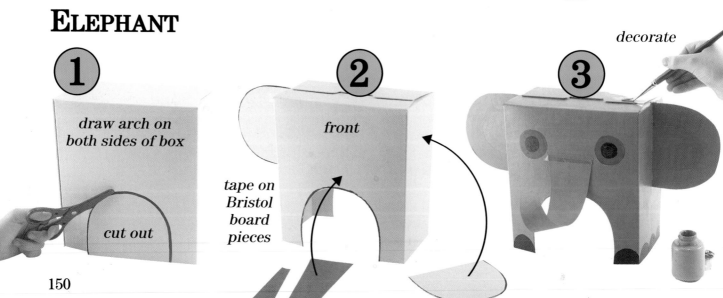

1

draw arch on both sides of box

cut out

2

front

tape on Bristol board pieces

3

decorate

HIPPO

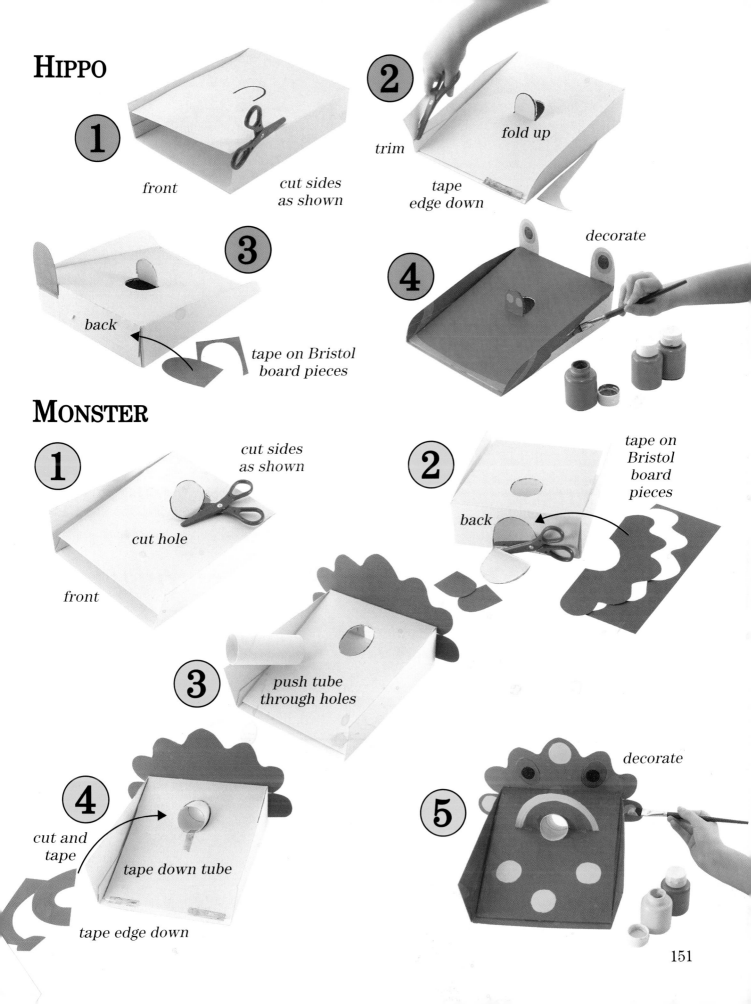

1 *front* — cut sides as shown

2 trim — *fold up* — tape edge down

3 back — tape on Bristol board pieces

4 decorate

MONSTER

1 cut sides as shown — *front* — cut hole

2 back — tape on Bristol board pieces

3 push tube through holes

4 cut and tape — tape down tube — tape edge down

5 decorate

151

CROCODILE

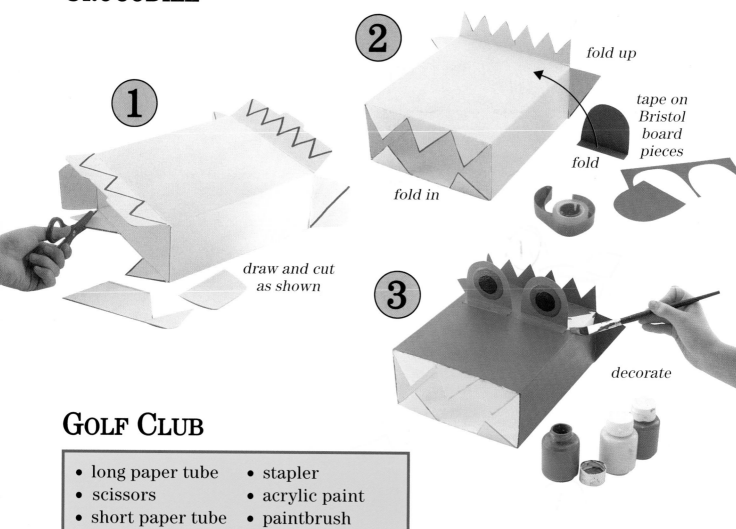

1 draw and cut as shown

2 fold up
fold in
fold
tape on Bristol board pieces

3 decorate

GOLF CLUB

- long paper tube
- scissors
- short paper tube
- stapler
- acrylic paint
- paintbrush

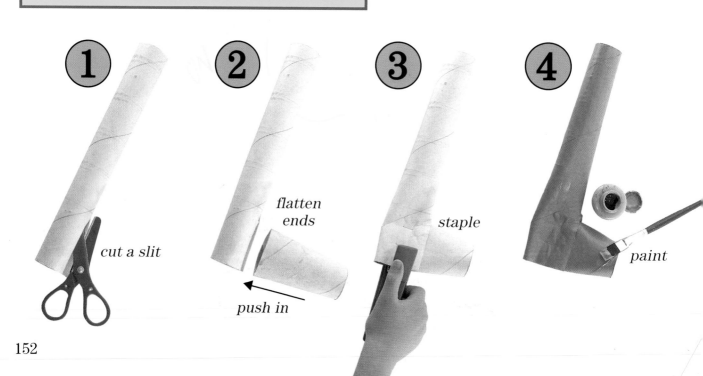

1 cut a slit

2 flatten ends
push in

3 staple

4 paint

CUP

- Bristol board
- scissors
- construction paper
- marker
- bendable straw
- tape

1 cut out center

cut circle from Bristol board

2 cut out four construction paper flags

number flags 1 to 4

3 tape

tape

bend straw

TEE

1 cut Bristol board circle

- Bristol board
- scissors
- egg carton
- tape
- acrylic paint
- paintbrush

2 cut and trim

3 tape down

4 decorate and dry

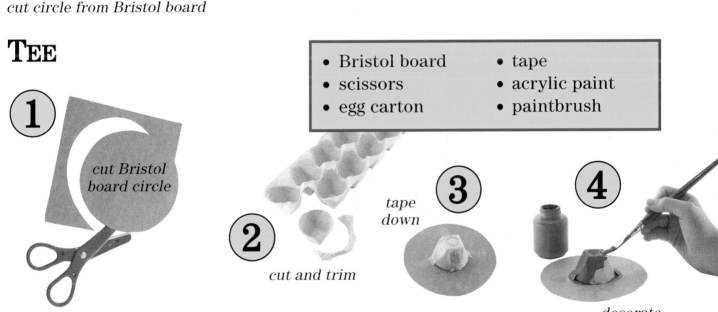

HOW TO PLAY

- Two or more play. Find a clear space for playing.
- Set up course: 1 tee, 1 hazard and 1 cup for each hole.
- Start by putting a small ball on the first tee. Hit the ball with golf club. Try to hit it through the hazard and then into the cup. Try to use as few hits as possible to get the ball into the cup.
- Your score is the number of hits it takes to get the ball in the cup.
- After everyone plays all four holes, total each player's scores. The lowest total score wins.

TREASURE HUNT

- *adult to give permission to dig*
- 2 brown paper bags
- soil
- water
- bowl
- plastic bag
- pencil crayons
- scissors
- envelope
- tape
- aluminum foil
- toy shovel
- treasure (candy, toys, books, etc.)

1 tear one bag into a flat piece for map

2 carefully tear other bag into pieces for clues

3 crinkle   smooth out

4 mix 2 spoons soil into a bowl of water

5 dip paper and let dry on plastic

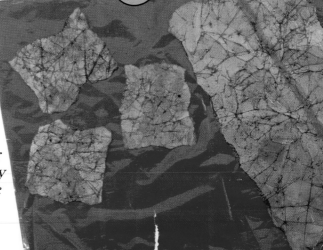

6 decide where to hide clues and treasure

draw a treasure map

7 write and number the clues

① Climb the stairs to where you sleep. On the floor you'll have to creep.

② Find the tree that has a split. Stand on your toes and reach for it.

③ Come out here to rest your feet. Look underneath this cosy red seat.

8 cut up the map

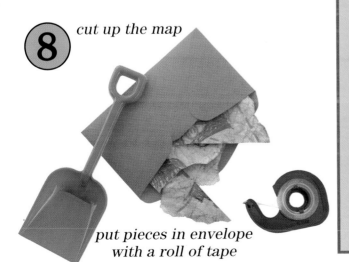

put pieces in envelope with a roll of tape

HOW TO PLAY
- Hide the treasure. If you want to bury it, wrap it in aluminum foil first. Get permission to dig.
- Hide map and clues #2 and #3. Clue #1 will lead to where clue #2 is. Clue #2 will lead to where clue #3 is. Clue #3 will lead to where the map is.
- Two or more play: treasure hider and one or more treasure hunters.
- Give clue #1 to the treasure hunters.
- The treasure hunters must find the clues in order, find the map, and then tape the map together. The map will lead the hunters to the treasure.

TRIP KIT

- *adult to help punch holes*
- shoe box with lid
- felt
- scissors
- white glue
- chalk
- fabric marker
- hole punch
- envelopes for storing pieces

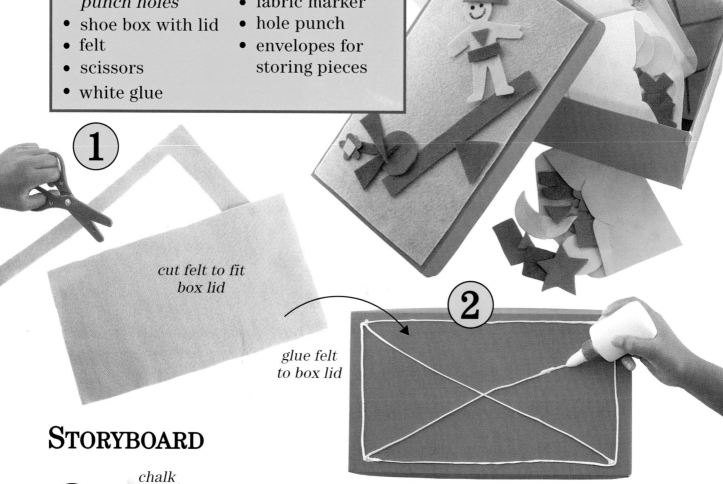

① cut felt to fit box lid

② glue felt to box lid

STORYBOARD

① chalk

② draw and cut shapes from felt

③ decorate

arrange pieces on box lid to make pictures and stories

156

Xs and Os

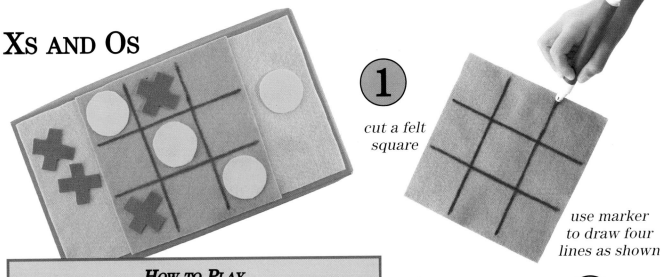

① cut a felt square

use marker to draw four lines as shown

How to Play
- Two people play.
- Place square on box lid.
- One player takes Xs; the other player takes Os. Take turns putting your pieces on empty spaces.
- Three in a row going any direction wins.

cut four circles for Os

② cut four squares and cut out corners for Xs

Solitaire

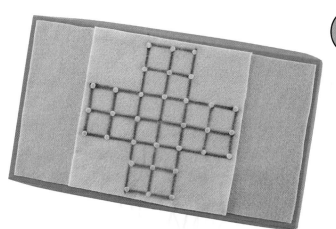

① cut felt square

draw lines as shown

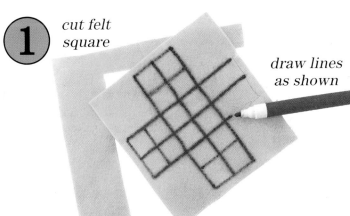

punch holes as shown

②

punch 32 circles of another color

How to Play
- One person can play.
- Place square on box lid.
- Put the felt circles into all the holes except the one in the center.
- At every move, jump one circle over one next to it, and remove the jumped circle. Keep jumping and removing circles until there are no jumps possible.
- End up with as few circles as you can.

If you've had fun reading *I Can Make That!*, here's a selection of other books from Maple Tree Press you'll also enjoy! For more information visit www.mapletreepress.com.

For kids ages 3–8

Before & After
by Jan Thornhill

The Nature Treasury: A First Look at the Natural World
by Lizann Flatt

Over in the Meadow
by Jan Thornhill

For kids ages 8–12

Are You Psychic?: The Official Guide for Kids
by Helaine Becker

Boredom Blasters: Brain Bogglers, Awesome Activities, Cool Comics, Tasty Treats, and More
and
Funny Business: Clowning Around, Practical Jokes, Cool Comedy, Cartooning, and More
by Helaine Becker

Cartooning for Kids
by Marge Lightfoot

Daniel's Dinosaurs: A True Story of Discovery
by Charles Helm

Ha! Ha! Ha!: 1000+ Jokes, Riddles, Facts, and More
by Lyn Thomas

What's the Matter with Albert?: A Story of Albert Einstein
by Frieda Wishinsky

Make Your Own Inuksuk
by Mary Wallace

Look for these and other award-winning Maple Tree Press titles at your neighborhood or on-line bookstore.